Bidpa'i

**The instructive and entertaining Fables of Pilpay**

An ancient Indian Philosopher

Bidpa'i

**The instructive and entertaining Fables of Pilpay**
*An ancient Indian Philosopher*

ISBN/EAN: 9783337079420

Printed in Europe, USA, Canada, Australia, Japan

Cover: Foto ©ninafisch / pixelio.de

More available books at **www.hansebooks.com**

# THE
## Inſtructive and Entertaining
# FABLES
### OF
# *PILPAY,*

AN

Ancient *Indian* PHILOSOPHER.

Containing a Number of excellent

# RULES

For the CONDUCT of Perſons of all Ages, and in all Stations: Under ſeveral Heads.

**THE SIXTH EDITION,**
Corrected, improved, and enlarged; and adorned with near ſeventy CUTS neatly engraved.

*Fable is not only the ſureſt Way of giving Council, but that which pleaſes the moſt univerſally.* ADDISON.
*After the ſacred Writings, there is no Work for which the World in general has paid ſo great an Eſteem as the Fables of* Pilpay. ——*They have been tranſlated into almoſt all the known Languages.* Dict. de MORERI.

*L O N D O N:*
Printed for J. F. and C. RIVINGTON, S. CROWDER, T. LONGMAN, B. LAW, S. BLADON, G. and T. WILKIE, and B. COLLINS.
M.DCCLXXXIX.

# PREFACE.

IT may not be improper to inform the reader, that the fables contained in this treatise, though but little known in our part of the world, are in many of the eastern nations, at this time, universally read, and esteemed an inestimable treasure of knowledge and instruction; and, that the author is so highly admired there, that Pilpay (for so he was called) is, with them, a name as much honoured as that of Æsop in many other nations.

This Pilpay was an Indian philosopher, a man of high rank in that nation, and of great renown for his wisdom throughout all the east; he was of that sect which the natives of those places call Bramins, a name, like that

## PREFACE.

of the Magi or Druids of some other nations, expressing, that those who are honoured with it are persons of extraordinary learning and wisdom.

This renowned philosopher composed this little work while he governed a part of Indostan, under the sovereignty of the most potent monarch Dabschelim. Pilpay has displayed all his wisdom in this little piece; and, according to the custom of the eastern people, who never teach but in parables, he here lays before all kings and princes the best and wisest methods of governing their subjects, couched under the disguise of histories of things which happened among birds and beasts, as well as those of his own species.

Dabschelim for a long time kept this work as a great secret, and left it as a most sacred treasure to his successors, among whom it remained, unknown to all the world beside, till the reign of Noufchirvan king of Persia.

This prince, who was a man of great wisdom and curiosity, having heard much talk of the book, sent his
prin-

# PREFACE

principal phyſician, a man in whoſe fidelity and addreſs he could confide, to the Indies, on purpoſe to procure a copy of it. The phyſician diſcharged himſelf of his truſt, to the great ſatisfaction of his maſter, brought him the book into Perſia, and, being a perſon who perfectly underſtood the Indian language, tranſlated the fables into the ancient Perſian tongue; and this was the firſt public edition of this moſt excellent work.

Many ages after this, the Arabians, after they had conquered the fineſt provinces of the eaſt, and begun to poliſh the rudeneſs of their manners with the ornaments of learning, not only endeavoured to render their language copious and delightful, but invited into their country the moſt wiſe and learned perſons of all the nations of the world; to whom they gave great rewards for tranſlating the moſt remarkable books of every country. And, at this time, Aboul Haſſan Abdalla Almanſor tranſlated theſe fables,

## PREFACE.

continued this manner of expreſſing their ſenſe, and unfolding their doctrines, that the eſteem, they had it in, cannot be concealed from thoſe who have peruſed their writings. In the Talmud, Bereſchit, Rabba, Zohar, &c. they make the waters, mountains, trees, and letters, themſelves to ſpeak.

The reſt of the orientals have in this alſo followed the example of the Hebrews; the Indians had our author; and the parables of Sandhaber are ſtill extant in the Hebrew. The Egyptians and Nubians have their Lochman, the moſt ancient of all the reſt, ſince Mirkhond in his firſt volume makes him cotemporary with David. And the Arabians alſo have a large book of fables, which is in great reputation among them; and the author of which is highly applauded by their falſe prophet.

The eſteem for this manner of writing became afterwards ſo great in the world, that the Greeks became imitators of the Eaſtern nations in it. And this cannot be doubted by any, ſince the Greeks themſelves acknowledge that they

they derived this sort of learning from Æsop, who was an oriental. Among the modern writers, the excellent Mr. Addison observes, 'That fables were 'the first pieces of wit that made 'their appearance in the world, and 'have been still highly valued, not on-'ly in times of the greatest simpli-'city, but among the most polite ages 'of mankind.' And in other places, 'That allegories, when well chosen, 'are like so many tracks of light in a 'discourse that make every thing about 'them clear and beautiful.' And even speaks with honour of that kind of writing, wherein the poet quite loses sight of nature, and entertains his readers imagination with characters and actions of such persons as have no existence but what the author bestows upon them. Let this justify our excellent author in his fable of the angel, ruler of the sea, and whatever other are his bolder passages.

That fable in general has been the most ancient of all ways of instructing is unquestionable; and it has always been so well received, that, to condemn it, is declaring against the common sense of mankind. Young people, as another very excellent author observes, are exceeding fond of fables; and it is good to take advantage of that fondness for honest purposes.

And the fables of this author have this particular advantage, that through the whole book one is made the introduction to another, in such manner, that it is not easy, when once entered on reading it, to leave off before the end of a chapter.

This has been by some objected to as a fault in the work; but I cannot help thinking that it is one of its greatest beauties. This manner of making one story introduce another has ever been admired as one of the greatest beauties of Ovid's Metamorphosis, and is plainly here of greater use, as in the works of this kind, of other authors, when a person has read one fable, which is a detached piece and has no dependence on the rest, he has done, and his mind is satisfied; whereas, here, when a young

young person has read one fable, the author has so contrived it, that his curiosity is excited to go through another, and so on to the end of that chapter; in which also, by the excellent contrivance of the author, the same set of morals are inculcated in a variety of beautiful relations.

But we shall now leave the reader to make his own reflections, observing only this in general, that one of the reasons which obliged the eastern people to make use of fables in their instructions and admonitions was, that, the eastern monarchies being for the most part absolute, their subjects were always restrained from freedom of speech. The result of which was, that, being an ingenious people, they found out this way, whereby they might be able, without exposing their lives to imminent danger, to inform and advise their princes of what most nearly concerned the welfare both of themselves and their subjects, and instruct them, without giving offence, in the paths of virtue, honour, and true glory.

GENERAL

# GENERAL HEADS.

INTRODUCTION,        Page 1

### CHAP. I.
*Fortune favours the bold,*     7

### CHAP. II.
*That we ought to avoid the Insinuations of Flatterers and Backbiters,*     39

### CHAP. III.
*That the Wicked come to an ill End,*     120

### CHAP. IV.
*How we ought to make Choice of Friends, and what Advantage may be reaped from their Conversation,*     158

### CHAP. V.
*That we ought always to distrust our Enemies, and be perfectly informed of what passes among them,*     188

# CONTENTS.

*WHAT* gave Occasion to the writing of this Book, and by whom it was composed, Page 1

## CHAP. I. FABLE I.
The story of Dabschelim *and* Pilpay, 7

### FABLE II.
The travelling Pidgeon, 17

### FABLE III.
The Falcon and the Raven, 23

### FABLE IV.
The greedy and ambitious Cat, 26

### FABLE V.
The poor man that became a King, 29

FABLE

# CONTENTS.

### FABLE VI.
The Leopard and the Lion,    34

---

## CHAP. II. FABLE I.
A Merchant and his lewd Children,    39

### FABLE II.
A King and his two Sons,    41

### FABLE III.
A Dervise, a Falcon, and a Raven,    44

### FABLE IV.
A Country-man and several Rats,    46

### FABLE V.
The Carpenter and the Ape,    50

### FABLE VI.
The two Travellers, and the Lion carved in Stone,    51

### FABLE VII.
The Fox and the Hen,    59

### FABLE VIII.
The Dervise that left his Habitation,    63

FABLE.

# CONTENTS.

### FABLE IX.
The Sparrow and the Sparrow-hawk, 71

### FABLE X.
A King who, from a Tyrant, became benign and just, 74

### FABLE XI.
A Raven, a Fox, and a Serpent, 76

### FABLE XII.
The Crane and the Cray-fish, 77

### FABLE XIII.
The Rabbit, the Fox, and the Wolf, 80

### FABLE XIV.
The Lion and the Rabbit, 82

### FABLE XV.
The two Fishermen and the three Fish, 87

### FABLE XVI.
The Scorpion and the Tortoise, 89

### FABLE XVII.
The Falcon and the Hen, 94

### FABLE XVIII.
The Nightingale and the Countryman, 95

FABLE.

# CONTENTS.

### FABLE XIX.
The Hunter, the Fox, and the Leopard, 97

### FABLE XX.
The Wolf, the Fox, the Raven, and the Camel, 98

### FABLE XXI.
The Angel, Ruler of the-Sea, and two Birds called Gerandi, 104

### FABLE XXII.
The Tortoise and two Ducks, 105

### FABLE XXIII.
The two young Merchants, the one crafty the other without Deceit. 109

### FABLE XXIV.
The Frog, the Cray-fish, and the Serpent, 111

### FABLE XXV.
The Gardener and the Bear, 114

### FABLE XXVI.
The Merchant and his Friend, 116

---

### CHAP. III. FABLE I.
The Fox, the Wolf, aud the Hen, 121

FABLE

# CONTENTS.

### FABLE II.
The Ass and the Gardener,     122

### FABLE III.
The Prince and his Minister,     125

### FABLE IV.
The Hermit who quitted the Desart to live at Court,     128

### FABLE V.
The blind Man who travelled with one of his Friends,     131

### FABLE VI.
The religious Doctor and the Dervise,     135

### FABLE VII.
The Merchant's Wife and the Painter,     139

### FABLE VIII.
The three envious Persons that found Money,     142

### FABLE IX.
The ignorant Physician,     147

### FABLE X.
The virtuous woman and the young Falconer,     152

CHAP.

# CONTENTS.

### CHAP. IV. FABLE I.

The Raven, the Rat, the Pidgeon, the Tortoise, and the Goat, — 159

### FABLE II.
The Partridge, and the Falcon, 163

### FABLE III.
The Man and the Adder, 166

### FABLE IV.
The Adventures of Zirac, 172

### FABLE V.
The Husband and his Wife, 174

### FABLE VI.
The Hunter and the Wolf, 175

### FABLE VII.
The ravenous Cat, 180

### FABLE VIII.
The two Friends, 181

---

### CHAP. V. FABLE I.
The Ravens and the Owls, 189

FABLE.

### FABLE II.
*The King and his Miſtreſs,*     193

### FABLE III.
*The original of the Hatred between the Ravens and the Owls,*     196

### FABLE IV.
*The Elephants and the Rabbits,*     198

### FABLE V.
*The Cat and the two Birds,*     203

### FABLE VI.
*The Derviſe and the four Robbers,*     206

### FABLE VII.
*The Merchant, his Wife, and the Robber,* 209

### FABLE VIII.
*The Derviſe, the Thief, and the Devil,* 211

### FABLE IX.
*The Joiner and his Wife,*     213

### FABLE X.
*The Monkeys and the bears,*     217

### FABLE XI.
*The Mouſe that was changed into a little Girl,*     226

FABLE

# CONTENTS.
## FABLE XII.
The serpent and the Frogs, 229

The Conclusion, 231

THE
# FABLES
OF
*PILPAY.*

## INTRODUCTION.

TOWARDS the eastern confines of China there once reigned a monarch, whose renown, as well for arms as wisdom and virtue, spread far and near, through all the countries of the east, and made him the admiration of all that part of the world. The greatest princes of the east were subject to his dominion, and admirers of his virtues. He was attended like Cohadan, and lodged like Poashti*; potent as Alexander, and armed like Darius. His council was composed of persons of inte-

* Cohadan and Poashti were two eastern princes; famous for their conquests and magnificence through all that part of the world.

grity

grity and learning; his riches were immense, his arms numerous, and himself both valiant and juſt. Rebels felt his anger, and his ſoldiers imitated his valour; his juſtice humbled the pride of tyrants, while his goodneſs ſuccoured the miſerable. In a word, under the empire of Humayon-Fal, (for ſo this virtuous prince was called,) the people were happy, becauſe every where, throughout his vaſt dominions, the moſt ſtrict ſearch was made after the wicked, and care was taken to puniſh them as enemies to the public tranquillity.

*Juſtice ought to be the rule of every prince's actions, who deſires his kingdom and his throne ſhould be eſtabliſhed like the reſidence of the Supreme; and whatever monarch omits to adminiſter puniſhments to vice, and rewards to virtue, let him be aſſured his dominions will not be long ſecure from ruin.*

Good kings generally make good ſervants; and ſo it happened to this excellent monarch; for, he had a vizir, or prime miniſter, who loved the people like a real father; he was merciful and compaſſionate; and his counſels, like tapers, gave light into the moſt hidden ſecrets. His name was Gnogeſtehrai, that is to ſay, ſucceſsful counſel, and very properly was he ſo called, ſince by his underſtanding he had rendered the king-

dom

dom happy. The king never undertook any enterprize without first consulting him. He did every thing by his advice; for, he found that without it nothing prospered.

It happened that once, as the monarch attended by this vizir had been hunting, after the pleasure and sport of their exercise were over, the king was for returning to his palace: but the heat of the sun was so violently scorching, that he told the vizir, he was not able to endure it: to which the vizir answered, that, if it were his majesty's pleasure, he might go to the foot of a certain neighbouring mountain where he would be sure of cool shade and the refreshing breezes of the wind; and there they might pleasantly spend the heat of the day. The king followed his advice, and in a little time they got to the place, where the coolness, caused by the shade of several trees that nature seemed to have taken delight to plant by the side of a number of winding brooks and fountains, made them forget the heat which they had endured upon the open road. The king, finding the covert very delightful, sat down upon the grass, and, falling into a contemplation of the works of the great Creator of all things, admired the inimitable painting of the flowers, and other productions of nature, that offered themselves to his sight.

As he was, with this most laudable view, looking about him, he spied at some little distance the trunk of a tree, which the rottenness of the wood declared to be decayed, and very old, in which there was a swarm of bees that were making honey: upon this, having never seen an object of this kind before, he could not avoid asking the vizir, what those little creatures were? Most sovereign monarch, replied that minister, those little creatures are very beneficial, and of a thousand uses in society; and are in the highest degree remarkable for the order of their government. They have a king among them, who is bigger than the rest, and whom they all obey; he resides in a little square apartment, and has his vizirs, his porters, his serjeants, and his guards; the industry of these, and all his other officers and people in general, is such, that they frame every one for themselves a little six-cornered chamber of wax, the angles of which differ not at all in shape or dimensions, but are so exactly made to answer one another, that the most expert geometrician could not range them with more regularity. These little chambers finished, the vizir takes of them an oath of fidelity that they are never to defile themselves: according to which promise, they never light but upon the branches of rose-bushes or
odoriferous

odoriferous flowers, so that their food which is aërial, and of the quintessence of flowers, is digested in a little time, and changed into a substance of a sweet and pleasing taste. When they return home, the porters smell to them, and if they have no ill scent about them they are permitted to enter; but if they have any ungrateful smell they kill them: or if they negligently suffer any one that has an ill scent to enter, and the king happens to smell it, he sends for the porters and puts them and the offender to death at the same time. If any strange fly endeavours to enter this community, the porters oppose him, and if he seeks to come in by violence he is put to death. Historians also report to us, great emperor! that Poashti learned to build his palace, to have vizirs, porters, guards, and officers, from these little creatures.

When the king had heard the vizir thus discourse, he went near the tree, stood still to behold the little animals at work, and, after he had well considered them, declared aloud his admiration to see a society of insects so well governed. His vizir, beholding him wrapt up in astonishment, addressed himself to him in this manner: Sir, said he, all this good order depends only upon the good counsel and prudent conduct of wise and able ministers, well affected to their prince and lovers of the public peace; thefe are the perfons that always preferve an empire in a flourifhing condition; and, whenever thefe things are mentioned, we ought to remember the ftrongeft inftance of this maxim ever known, which was in the conduct of the great Dabfchelim, who wholly intrufted the government of his kingdoms to the good counfels of that miracle of wifdom, the bramin Pilpay; infomuch that, by the guidance of that minifter, he reigned in peace, and the greateft profperity and earthly happinefs, while he lived, and, dying, left to his pofterity a name, for ever to be remembered with efteem and honour.

When the king heard him pronounce the names of Dabfchelim and Pilpay, he felt in himfelf the motions of a more than ordinary joy. I have, faid he to the vizir, for a long time moft earneftly defired to hear the ftory of that bramin's government, but never yet could meet with an opportunity to fatisfy myfelf, nor ever imagined that you knew their hiftory. I am now more happy than I could expect, and defire you will immediately relate to me the ftory, that my kingdom may be eftablifhed in happinefs by the maxims of that venerable philofopher. On this command of the monarch the vizir thus entered on the hiftory.

C H A P.

# CHAP. I.

FORTUNE *favours* the BOLD.

*The story of* DABSCHELIM *and* PILPAY.

ON the banks of the Indus, towards the sea-coast, and over a vast extent of country thereabouts, there reigned a prince, whose ministers (persons of justice, wisdom, and understanding) by their counsels rendered the subjects happy, and always successfully brought to pass the just designs of the sovereign. This excellent prince was an enemy of oppression; nor could the wicked ever gain their ends in his dominions. He was called Dabschelim; (a name most proper for such a prince, as signifying, in their language, a *great king*). His puissance was such, that he undertook none but extraordinary enterprizes, and those always just, and on honest and honourable grounds; to relieve the distressed or punish the proud oppressor were the only occasions of his entering on war. His army was composed of ten thousand elephants; valiant and experienced

experienced soldiers he had about him in great numbers, and his treasures were kept full to support them. This rendered him formidable to his enemies, and procured the repose of his people, of whom he took a particular care; hearing their complaints and differences, composing their quarrels, and making himself the arbitrator of their disputes, without any respect to his greatness or superior rank. He never forsook the interests of his people, but referred their affairs, when of too long and intricate a nature to come under his own cognizance, to the debates and decisions of men of justice and equity. When he had taken this good order for the government of his dominions, he lived in tranquillity, and spent his days with happiness and content. It happened that this wise and glorious monarch, one day, when he had been for a long time entertained with divers discourses upon the several sciences, and the use they and the principles of equity and honour must be of in the well governing a people, laid himself down upon his bed to give some relaxation to his mind; which he had no sooner done, but he saw in a dream a figure full of light and majesty, which approaching toward him with a look of benevolence, and the highest favour, spoke in the following manner: *You have done this day as a good prince ought to do, and you shall be rewarded for it. To-morrow, by break of day, get on horseback, and ride toward the east, where you shall find an inestimable treasure, by the means of which you shall, as you deserve, exceed in glory and honour all other men.* Immediately the figure disappeared, and Dabschelim, awaking with a heart full of joy and gratitude, mounted one of his best horses, and rode

rode directly eastward. He passed in his way through several inhabited places, but at length arrived in a defart, where viewing the country, and casting his eyes on every side, to discover his expected happiness, he perceived, at a little distance before him, a mountain that reached above the clouds, at the foot of which he spied a cave, obscure, dark, and black, within, as the hearts of wicked men. Without it he saw sitting a man, whose aspect sufficiently shewed the austerity of his life. The king had a great desire to ride up to him, when the old man understanding his intention, came forward, and, breaking silence, addressed himself to the monarch in these words: Sir, said he, though my small cottage be nothing like to your magnificent palace, yet it is an ancient custom for kings, out of their goodness, to come and visit the poor. The looks of great men, cast down upon the mean, augment their own grandeur. I joy to see the greatest and the wisest monarch in the east not forget this ancient custom. And, O supreme and magnificent prince, let it not raise a blush in thee to cast thy royal looks on my low estate, when thou rememberest that Solomon, in the midst of all his glory and magnificence, vouchsafed to cast his eyes upon the little ants.

Dabschelim was pleased with the old man's civility, and alighted from his horse to discourse with him. After he had talked to him of divers things, as he was going to take his leave, the venerable sage surprized him with the following words: Sir, said he, it is not for a poor man, as I am, to offer any refreshment to so great a prince as you; but, permit me to tell you that I have a present, if your majesty pleases to accept it, which has descended to me from father to son, and which is appointed for you; it is a treasure which I have here by me, though I know not myself exactly the place where it now lies; but, if your majesty thinks it worth your acceptance, command your servants to seek for it. Dabschelim, hearing these words, recounted his dream to the good old man, who rejoiced extremely to find that his intentions in bestowing his treasure were conformable to the will of the supreme Power by whom he was intrusted with it.

The king now commanded his servants to search for the treasure round about the cave, and in a little time they discovered it, and brought before the king a vast number of chests and coffers, full of gold, silver, and jewels. Among the rest, there was one chest of a smaller size than the others, which was bound about with several bars of iron, and fastened with a multitude of padlocks, the keys of which were not to be found, notwithstanding all the care and diligence that was used to seek them. This highly increased the monarch's curiosity. There must be something, said he, in this little casket, much more precious than jewels, since it is so strongly and carefully barred and locked. A smith was now procured; and, the casket being broke open, there was found within it another small trunk of gold, set all over with precious stones, and within that yet another less box; this the king ordered to be delivered into his own hands. When this little box was opened, he found therein a piece of white satin, upon which were written some lines in the Syriac language. Dabschelim was astonish-

ed

ed at the accident, and in great perplexity to know what the words might signify. Some said it was the will of the owner of the treasure; and others, that it was a talisman, or some charm, for the preservation of it. After every one had delivered his opinion, it was the king's pleasure that enquiry should be made for some person who was able to interpret the meaning of the lines; and, after long search, a person was found who perfectly understood all the oriental languages, who, when he had looked over it, said to the king, Sir, this writing is, to a prince, indeed an inestimable treasure; it contains the rules, admonitions, and instructions, of a great king, for the well governing a people; and how nearly it particularly concerns yourself, O king! permit me to shew, by reading to you what it contains. The king bidding him read aloud, he then began as follows.

*The writing of the great King* Houschenk, *left with his treasures.*

I King Houschenk, have disposed of this treasure, for the use of the great king Dabschelim, understanding, by a visionary revelation, him to be the person for whom it was designed; and, among the precious stones, I have concealed this my last will and testament, by way of instruction to him, to let him know that it is not for men of reason and understanding to be dazz'ed with the lustre of glittering treasures. Riches are but borrowed conveniences, and are to be repaid to our successors. The pleasures of this world are charming, but they are not eternal. This testament is a

thing

thing of much more real use than all these treasures: it is an abridgement of the good rules proper to regulate the conduct of kings; and he must, be a wise prince who regulates his conduct by these instructions, which are in number fourteen.

I. *That he never discard his domestic servants at the solicitation of other persons.* For, he, that is near the person of a king, will never want some who will be envious and jealous of his happiness; and when they see that the king has any affection for him, will not cease, by a thousand calumnies, if it can be done, to render him odious to his master.

II. *That he never suffer in his presence flatterers nor railers;* for, these people are always seeking occasions of disturbance. It is better to exterminate such people from the earth than to let them be a trouble to human society.

III. *That he always preserve his ministers and grandees, if it be possible, in a right understanding with one another*; to the end that they may unanimously labour for the good and welfare of the state.

IV. *That he never trust to the submissions of his enemies.* The more affections they testify, and the louder protestations they make of their services, the more artifices and villanies are to be mistrusted in them. *There is no relying upon the friendship of an enemy*; he is to be shunned, when he approaches with the countenance of a friend, as the syren who puts on charms but with an intent to destroy.

V. *When a man has once acquired what he has diligently sought after, let him preserve it carefully; for, we have not every day the same opportunity to gain*

*gain what we desire.* And, when we have not preserved what we have once acquired, we have nothing left us but the vexation of having lost it. *We cannot fetch the arrow back which we have once let fly, though we should eat our fingers for madness.*

VI. *That we never ought to be too hasty in business;* but, on the other side, before we put any enterprize in execution, it behoveth us to weigh and examine what we are going to do. Things done in haste, and with a precipitate rashness, come frequently to a mischievous conclusion. He repents in vain who cannot recal what he has done amiss.

VII. *That a man never despise good counsel, and prudence.* If there be a necessity for him to make peace with his enemies, in order to deliver himself out of their hands, let him do it without delay.

VIII. *To avoid the company of dissemblers, and never to hearken to their smooth speeches;* for, as in their bosoms they carry nothing but the plants of enmity, they can never bring forth the fruits of friendship.

IX. *To be merciful.* Never let a monarch inflict a punishment on his subjects or servants for faults committed through infirmity: for, a merciful prince upon earth is an angel in heaven. We ought to consider the weakness of men, and, in charity and goodness, to conceal their defects. Subjects have always committed faults, and kings have always pardoned them, when they have only committed the faults which the common frailties of human nature have betrayed them into.

X.

X. *Not to procure the harm or injury of any person.* On the other hand, we ought to do our neighbour all the good we can. *If you do good, good will be done to you; but, if you do evil, the same will be measured back to you again.*

XI. *That a king seek not after any thing that may be below his dignity, or a subject what is contrary to his genius or nature.* There are many persons who let alone their own affairs to intrude themselves into other people's business, and at last do nothing at all. The crow would needs learn to fly like the partridge; it was a way of flying which he could never attain, and, in attempting to learn it, he forgot his own.

XII. *To be of a mild and affable temper.* Mildness, in society, is like salt in our food: as salt seasons and gives a relish to all meat, the other gives content to every body. The sword of steel is not so sharp as the sword of mildness; it vanquishes even invincible armies.

XIII. *For a king to seek out faithful ministers, and never to admit, into his service or councils, knaves and deceivers.* By wise and honest ministers the kingdom will be kept safe, and the king's secrets will never be revealed.

XIV. *Never to be disturbed at the accidents of the world.* A man of resolution and true courage suffers all adversities with a settled fortitude, and relies upon the providence of heaven, while a fool minds nothing but his pastime and his pleasure.

There are several fables of excellent instructions founded on every one of these heads, which
if

if the king will hear, he muſt go to the mountain Serandib\*, which was the manſion of our fathers, and there all the hiſtories compoſed to illuſtrate and explain theſe admonitions will be related to him, and every queſtion that can come into his heart to aſk, concerning the making his people happy, will be anſwered as from an oracle of heaven.

When the learned man had done reading, Dabſchelim caught him in his arms and eagerly embraced him; and having received back again the piece of ſatin, which he took with the moſt profound reſpect, he tied it about his arm, ſaying at the ſame time, I was promiſed indeed a worldly treaſure, but beſide I have found a treaſure of ſecrets. Heaven has favoured me with plenty of its bleſſings, for which my grateful ſoul now offers its moſt humble adorations and praiſes. Having ſaid this, he ordered the gold and ſilver to be diſtributed to the poor, and returned to his palace, where all that night he did nothing but ruminate upon the journey which he was to make to Serandib.

The next morning, by ſun-riſe, Dabſchelim ſent for two of his principal miniſters, in whom he had a great confidence: to theſe he diſcovered his dream, and what had afterwards befallen him, and told them he had a moſt earneſt inclination to make a journey to Serandib. I have for a long time, ſaid he, taken this courſe, to adviſe with my council before I undertook any of my enter-

---

\* A vaſt mountain, famous for the reſidence of many of the learned men of the eaſt.

prizes, and in this alfo I am willing to refer myself to your judgements. And now I have told you my intentions, and the reafon of them, I conjure you by your honours, and the efteem I have for you, to tell me what you think, as a prince who knows his duty to be the care of his fubjects, I ought to do on this occafion. The two minifters defired the remainder of the day and the night following to confider the whole matter, that they might not without due deliberation give their anfwer in a thing of fo high concernment. Dabfchelim granted their requeft, and the next day they came to wait upon the king; and, every one being feated in their places, fo foon as the monarch made them the fign to fpeak, the grand vizir fell upon his knees and thus began.

*Sir, in my opinion this journey is like to be more painful than profitable. Your majefty is to confider, that the perfon, who undertakes long journeys, renounces at the fame time his repofe; add to this, your majefty is not ignorant of the dangers and hazards to which the roads are fubject. It is not for a perfon of difcretion to change his quiet and eafe for labour and difturbance. Permit me on this occafion to call to your majefty's remembrance the fable of the pidgeon that would needs be a traveller, and the dangers which he met with.*

FABLE

# FABLE I.

### *The* TRAVELLING PIDGEON.

THERE were once, in a certain part of your majesty's dominions, two pidgeons, a male and a female, which had been hatched from the same brood of eggs, and bred up together afterwards in the same nest, under the roof of an old building, in which they lived together, in mutual content and perfect happiness, safely sheltered from all the injuries of the weather, and contented with a little water and a few tares. *It is a treasure to live in a desart when we enjoy the happiness of a friend; and there is no loss in quitting, for the sake of such an one, all other company in the world.* But it seems too often the peculiar business of destiny to separate friends. Of these pidgeons the one was called the Beloved, the other the Lover. One day the Lover, having an eager desire to travel, imparted his design to his companion. Must we always, said he, live confined to a hole? no! be it with you as you please, but for my part I am resolved to take a tour about the world: travellers every day meet with new things, and acquire experience; and all the great and learned among our ancestors have told us, that travelling is the only means to acquire knowledge. *If the sword be never unsheathed, it can never shew the valour of the person that wears it; and if the pen takes not its run through the extent of a page, it can never shew the eloquence of the author that uses it.* The heavens,

heavens, by reason of their perpetual motion, exceed in glory and delight the regions beneath them; and the dull brute earth is the solid place for all creatures to tread upon, only because it it is immoveable: if a tree could remove itself from one place to another, it would neither be afraid of the saw or the wedge, nor exposed to the ill-usage of the wood-mongers.

All this is true, said the Beloved; but, my dear companion, you know not, nor have you ever yet undergone, the fatigues of travel, nor do you understand what it is to live in foreign countries; and, believe me, travelling is a tree, the chiefest fruit of which is labour and disquiet. If the fatigues of travelling are very great, answered the Lover, they are abundantly rewarded with the pleasure of seeing a thousand rarities; and, when people are once grown accustomed to labour, they look upon it to be no hardship.

Travelling, replied the Beloved, my dear companion, is never delightful but when we travel in company of our friends; for, when we are are at a far distance from them, besides that we are exposed to the injuries of the weather, we are grieved to find ourselves separated from what we love: therefore take, my dearest, the advice which my tenderness suggests to you: never leave the place where you live at ease, nor forsake the object of your dearest affection.

If I find these hardships insupportable, replied the Lover, believe me I will return in a little time: if I do not, be assured that I am happy, and let the consciousness of that make you so also. After they had thus reasoned the case together, they went to their rest, and, meeting the next morning, the Lover being immoveable in his resolution, took their leaves of each other, and so parted.

The Lover left his hole like a bird that had made his escape out of a cage; and, as he went on his journey, was ravished with delight at the prospect of the mountains, rivers, and gardens, which he flew over; and, arriving towards evening at the foot of a little hill, where several rivulets, shaded with lovely trees, watered the enamelled meadows, he resolved to spend the night in a place that so effectually resembled a terrestrial paradise. But, alas! how soon began he to feel the vicissitudes of fortune! hardly had he betaken himself to his repose upon a tree, when the air grew gloomy, and blazing gleams of lightening began to flash against his eyes, while the thunder rattled along the plains, and became doubly terrible by its echoes from the neighbouring mountains. The rain also and the hail came down together in whole torrents, and made the poor pidgeon hop from bow to bow, beaten, wetted to the skin, and in continual terror of being consumed in a flash of lightning. In short, he spent the night so ill, that he already heartily repented having left his comrade.

The next morning, the sun having dispersed the clouds, the Lover was prudent enough to take his leave of the tree, with a full resolution to make the best of his way home again; he had not however flown fifty yards, when a sparrow-hawk, with a keen appetite, perceiving our traveller, pursued him upon the wing. The pidgeon, seeing him at a distance, began to tremble; and, as he approached nearer, utterly despairing e-
ver

ver to see his friend again, and no less sorry that he had not followed her advice, protested that, if ever he escaped that danger, he would never more think of travelling. In this time the sparrow-hawk had overtaken, and was just ready to seize, him, and tear him in pieces, when a hungry eagle, lancing down with a full stoop upon the sparrow-hawk, cried out, hold, let me devour that pidgeon, to stay my stomach till I find something else more solid. The sparrow-hawk however, no less courageous than hungry, would not, though unequal in strength, give way to the eagle, so that the two birds of prey fell to fighting one with another, and in the mean time the poor pidgeon escaped, and, perceiving a hole so small that it would hardly give entrance to a titmouse, yet made shift to squeeze himself into it, and so spent the night in a world of fear and trouble. By break of day he got out again, but he was now become so weak for want of food that he could hardly fly; add to this, he had not yet half recovered himself from the fear he was in the day before: as he was however full of terror, looking around about him to see whether the sparrow-hawk or the eagle appeared, he spied a pidgeon in a field, at a small distance, with a great deal of corn scattered in the place where he was feeding. The Lover rejoiced at the sight, drew near this happy pidgeon, as he thought him, and, without compliments, fell to: but he had hardly pecked three grains before he found himself caught by the legs. *The pleasures of this world, indeed, are generally but snares which the devil lays for us.*

Brother,

Brother, said the Lover to the other pidgeon, we are both of one and the same species; wherefore then did not you inform me of this piece of treachery, that I might not have fallen into these springes they have laid for us. To which the other answered, forbear complaints, nobody can prevent his destiny; nor can all the prudence of man preserve him from inevitable accidents. The Lover, on this, next besought him to teach him some expedient to free himself from the danger that threatened him. Poor innocent creature, answered the other, if I knew any means to do this, dost thou not think I would make use of it to deliver myself, that so I might not be the occasion of surprizing others of my fellow-creatures? alas! unfortunate friend, thou art but like the young camel, who, weary with travelling, cried to his mother, with tears in his eyes, O mother without affection! stop a little, that I may take breath and rest myself: to whom the mother replied, O son without consideration! seest thou not that my bridle is in the hand of another? were I at liberty, I would gladly both throw down my burden, and give thee my assistance: but, alas! we must both submit to what we cannot avoid or prevent. Our traveller perceiving, by this discourse, that all hopes of relief from others were vain, resolved to rely only on himself, and, strengthened by his own despair, with much striving and long fluttering at length broke the snare, and, taking the benefit of his unexpected good fortune, bent his flight toward his own country; and, such was his joy for having escaped so great a danger, that he even forgot his hunger. However, at length, passing through a village, and

lighting,

lighting, merely for a little reft, upon a wall that was over againſt a field newly ſown, a countryman, that was keeping the birds from his corn, perceiving the pidgeon, flung a ſtone at him, and, while the poor Lover was dreaming of nothing leſs than of the harm that was ſo near him, hit him ſo terrible a blow that he fell quite ſtunned into a deep and dry well, that was at the foot of the wall. By this, however, he eſcaped being made the countryman's ſupper, who, not being able to come at his prey, left it in the well, and never thought more of it. There the pidgeon remained all the night long, with a ſad heart, and a wing half broken. During the night his misfortunes would not permit him to ſleep, and a thouſand and a thouſand times he wiſhed himſelf at home with his friend; the next day, however, he ſo beſtirred himſelf, that he got out of the well, and towards evening arrived at his old habitation.

The Beloved, hearing the fluttering of her companion's wings, flew forth with a more than ordinary joy to meet him; but, ſeeing him ſo weak and in ſo bad a condition, aſked him tenderly the reaſon of it; upon which the Lover told her all his adventures, proteſting heartily to take her advice for the future, and never to travel more.

I have recited, continued the vizir, this example to your majeſty, to diſſuade you from preferring the inconveniences of travelling to the repoſe that you enjoy at home, among the praiſes and adorations of a loyal and happy people. Wiſe vizir, ſaid the king, I acknowledge it a painful thing to travel; but it is no leſs true, that there is great and uſeful knowledge to be gained by it.

Should

Should a man be always tied to his own house or his own country, he would be deprived of the sight and enjoyment of an infinite number of noble things. And, to continue your allegoric history of birds, the falcon is happy in seeing the beauties of the world, while princes frequently carry them upon their hands, and for that honour and pleasure he quits the inglorious life of the nest. On the other hand, the owl is contemned, because he always hides himself in ruinous buildings and dark holes, and delights in nothing but retirement. The mind of man ought to fly abroad, and soar like the falcon, not hide itself like the owl. He that travels renders himself acceptable to all the world, and men of wisdom and learning are pleased with his conversation. Nothing is more clear and limpid than running water, while stagnating puddles grow thick and muddy. Had the famous falcon, that was bred in the raven's nest, never flown abroad, he would never have been so highly advanced. *The vizir on this humbly besought the king to recite that fable, which he did in the following manner.*

## FABLE II.

### The FALCON and the RAVEN.

THERE were once two falcons which had built their nests near one another in a very high mountain, whence they flew every way round them to seek food for their young ones. One day, as they were flown abroad upon the same design, they staid from their nests a little too long; for, in the mean time, one of the young ones, very hungry, put his head so far out of the nest to look for them, that he tumbled over, and fell from the top to the foot of the mountain; at this instant a raven, that happened to be in that part, met with the fallen youngling, and at first took it for a rat which some other raven had accidentally let fall; but, on more examination, finding by his beak and his talons that he was a bird of prey, he began to have a kindness for him; and, looking upon himself as an instrument ordained by heaven to save the helpless creature, carried it to his own nest, and bred it up with his own young ones, where the falcon grew every day bigger and bigger; and, coming at length to be of age to make reflections, nobly began to say to himself, If I am brother to these ravens, why am I not made as they are? and, if I am not of their race and progeny, why do I tarry here? One day as he was taken up with these meditations, Son, said the raven to him, I have observed thee for some time to be very sad and pensive; I conjure thee, let me know the cause of it: if any thing grieve thee, conceal it not from me, for I will endeavour thy relief and consolation. I know not myself, replied the falcon, the reason of my desires, but I have long resolved to beg your permission to travel. O son, cried the raven, thou art forming a design in thy young imagination, which my riper years can inform thee will create in thee an infinite deal of pains and danger. *Travelling is a sea that swallows up all the world.* Wise people, however, never travel,

vel, unless it be either to get great estates, or because they cannot live contented and easy at home: neither of these two reasons, thanks to heaven, can, I think, have infused this design into thy brain, because thou wantest for nothing; and why therefore wouldst thou leave us? thou hast the absolute power over thy brothers and sisters, and all that I can do for thee thou needest but command. It is a great folly, therefore, in thee to quit an assured repose at home to ramble in search of trouble and disquiet in foreign countries. To this the falcon replied, sir, what you tell me is most true, and I take it as a demonstration of your paternal kindness for me; but I feel something within me, which persuades me that I lead a life here, in this place, not worthy of myself. The raven on this could not but observe, that, in despite of a bad education, persons nobly descended are still the masters of sentiments becoming their birth. He would fain, however, have put him upon farther discourse, in hopes to wean him from this strong inclination to travel; and to that purpose, Son, said he, my exhortations are persuasions to sobriety and contentedness; but those high-soaring thoughts of thine are only the effects of avarice. And let me assure thee of this, *that whoever is not contented with what he has can never be at quiet in his mind*; and I am in the highest degree concerned to find thou art not satisfied with thy condition; but take with thee this my friendly admonition: beware lest what once befel the greedy and ambitious cat should happen to thee also. *The Story is this.*

C                    FABLE

## FABLE III.

*The greedy and ambitious* CAT.

THERE was formerly an old woman in a village, extremely thin, half starved, and meagre. . She lived in a little cottage as dark and gloomy as a fool's heart, and withal as close shut up as a miser's hand. This miserable creature had, for the companion of her wretched retirement, a cat, meagre and lean as herself; the poor creature never saw bread, nor beheld the face of a stranger, and was forced to be contented with only smelling the mice in their holes, or seeing the prints of their feet in the dust. If by some extraordinary lucky chance this miserable animal happened to catch a mouse, she was like a beggar that discovers a treasure; her visage and her eyes were inflamed with joy, and that booty served her for a whole week; and, out of the excess of her admiration and distrust of her own happiness, she would cry out to herself, Heavens! is this a dream, or is it real? One day, however, ready to die for hunger, she got upon the ridge of her enchanted castle, which had long been the mansion of famine for cats, and spied thence another cat, that was stalking upon a neighbour's wall like a lion, walking along as if she had been counting her steps, and so fat that she could hardly go. The old woman's cat, astonished to see a creature of her own species so plump and so large, with a loud voice cries out to her pursy neighbour, in the name of pity, *speak to me, thou happiest of the cat-kind!* Why, you look as if you came from one of the

khan

khan\* of Kathai's feasts; I conjure you, to tell me how, or in what region, it is that you get your skin so well stuffed? Where, replied the fat one? why, where should one feed well but at a king's table? I go to the house, continued she, every day about dinner-time, and there I lay my paws upon some delicious morsel or other, which serves me till the next, and then leave enough for an army of mice, which, under me, live in peace and tranquillity; for, why should I commit murder for a piece of tough and skinny mouse-flesh, when I can live on venison at a much easier rate? The lean cat on this eagerly enquired the way to this house of plenty, and intreated her plump neighbour to carry her one day along with her. Most willingly, said the fat puss, for, thou seest I am naturally charitable, and thou art so lean that I heartily pity thy condition. On this promise they parted; and the lean cat returned to the old woman's chamber, where she told her dame the story of what had befallen her. The old woman prudently endeavoured to dissuade her cat from prosecuting her design, admonishing her withal to have a care of being deceived; for, believe me, said she, *the desires of the ambitious are never to be satiated but when their mouths are stuffed with the dirt of their graves.* Sobriety and temperance are the only things that truly enrich people. I must tell thee, poor silly cat, that they, who travel to satisfy their ambition, have no knowledge of the good things they possess, *nor are they truly thankful to heaven for what they enjoy who are not contented with their fortune.*

---

\* A nobleman of the east, famous for his hospitality.

The poor starved cat, however, had conceived so fair an idea of the king's table, that the old woman's good morals and judicious remonstrances entered in at one ear and went out at the other; in short, she departed the next day with the fat puss to go to the king's house; but, alas! before she got thither, her destiny had laid a snare for her; for, being a house of good cheer, it was so haunted with cats, that the servants had, just at this time, orders to kill all the cats that came near it, by reason of a great robbery committed the night before, in the king's larder, by several grimalkins. The old woman's cat, however, pushed on by hunger, entered the house, and no sooner saw a dish of meat unobserved by the cooks, but she made a seizure of it, and was doing what for many years she had not done before, that is, heartily filling her belly; but, as she was enjoying herself under the dresser-board, and feeding heartily upon her stolen morsels, one of the testy officers of the kitchen, missing his breakfast, and seeing where the poor cat was solacing herself with it, threw his knife at her with such an unlucky hand, that he struck her full in the breast. However, as it has been the providence of nature to give this creature nine lives instead of one, poor puss made a shift to crawl away, after she had for some time shammed dead; but, in her flight, observing the blood come streaming from her wound; Well, said she, let me but escape this accident, and, if ever I quit my old hold and my own mice for all the rarities in the king's kitchen, may I lose all my nine lives at once!

I cite you this example, to shew you, that it is better to be contented with what one has than to travel in search of what ambition prompts us to seek for. What you say, said the falcon, is true, and it is very wholesome advice; but it is for mean and low spirits only to confine themselves always to a little hole. He that aspires to be a king must begin with the conquest of a kingdom, and he that would meet a crown must go in search of it. An effeminate and lazy life can never agree with a great soul.

You are very magnanimous, son, replied the raven, and, I perceive, design great conquests; but let me tell you, your enterprise cannot so soon be put in execution: before you can conquer a kingdom, you must get together arms and armies, and make great preparations. My talons, replied the falcon, are instruments sufficient to bring about my design, and myself am equal to the undertaking. Sure you never heard the story of the warrior, who by his single valour became a king! No, replied the raven; therefore, let me hear it from you: on which, the falcon related it in this manner.

## FABLE IV.

*The* POOR MAN *who became a* GREAT KING.

IT being the pleasure of heaven to rescue from misery a man who lived in extreme poverty, providence gave him a son, who from his infancy shewed signal signs that he would one day

day come to be a great man. This infant became an immediate blessing to the old man's house; for, his wealth increased, from day to day, from the time that the child was born. So soon as this young one could speak, he talked of nothing but swords, and bows and arrows. The father sent him to school, and did all he could to infuse into him a good relish of learning; but he neglected his book, and devoted his thoughts to nothing but running at the ring, and other warlike exercises with the other children.

When he came to years of discretion, Son, said his father to him, thou art now past the age of childhood, and art in the greatest danger to fall into disorder and irregularity, if thou givest thyself over to thy passions. I therefore intend to prevent that accident by marrying thee betimes. Dear father, replied the stripling, for heaven's sake refuse me not the mistress which my youthful years have already made choice of. Who is that mistress? presently replied the old man, with great earnestness and uneasiness, (for he had already looked out for him the daughter of a neighbouring hind, and agreed the matter with her father,) and what is her condition? This is she, the lad made answer, shewing his father a very noble sword; and by virtue of this I expect to become master of a throne. The father gave him many reasons to imagine he disapproved his intentions, and looked on them as little better than madness: many a good lecture followed during the remainder of the day; to avoid which, for the future, the young hero the next morning quitted his father's house, and travelled in search of opportunities to signalize

his

his courage. Many years he warred under the command of different monarchs: at length, after he had every where fignalized himfelf, not only by his conduct but by his perfonal courage, a neighbouring monarch, who, with his whole family, lay befieged in a fmall fortrefs, fent to him, to entreat him to accept of the command of all his forces, to get them together, and endeavour to raife the fiege, and relieve them; in which, if he fucceeded, he would make him his adopted fon, and the heir of his vaft empire. Our young warrior engaged in this, raifed a vaft army, fought the befiegers in their trenches, entirely conquered them, and was the gainer of a glorious victory: but, alas! the heat of the action made him not perceive that the fortrefs, in which the king was, was in flames; fome treacherous perfons had fired it at the inftigation of the general of the befieger's army, and the king and his whole family perifhed in the flames. The old monarch juft lived, however, to fee his deliverer, and to fettle on him the inheritance of his crown. The royal family being all extinct by this fatal calamity, the nobles ratified the grant, and our illuftrious hero lived many years a great and glorious monarch.

I have recited this example, faid the falcon to the raven, that you may underftand that I alfo find myfelf born to undertake great enterprizes: I have a ftrange foreboding within me, that I fhall prove no lefs fortunate than this famous warrior; and, for this reafon, can never quit my defign. When the raven perceived him fo fixed in his refolution, he confented to his putting it in execution: perfuaded that fo noble a courage would never be guilty of idle or unworthy actions.

The falcon having taken his leave of the raven, and bid farewel to all his pretended brethren, left the neft and flew away. Long he continued flying and in love with liberty; and, at length, ſtopt upon a mountain: here, looking round about him, he ſpied a partridge, in the fallow grounds, that made all the neighbouring hills refound with her note. Prefently the falcon lanced himſelf upon her, and, having got her in his pounce, began to tear and eat her. This is no bad beginning, ſaid he to himſelf; though it were for nothing but to tafte fuch delicate food, it is better travelling than to lie ſleeping in a nafty neft, and feed upon carrion as my brothers do. Thus he ſpent three days in careffing himſelf with delicate morſels; but, on the fourth, being upon the top of another mountain, he ſaw a company of men that were hawking; thefe happened to be the king of the country with all his court; and, while he was gazing upon them, he faw their falcon in purfuit of a heron. Upon that, pricked forward by a noble emulation, he flies with all his force, gets before the king's falcon, and overtakes the heron. The king, admiring this agility, commands his falconers to make ufe of all their cunning to catch this noble bird, which by good luck they did. And in a little time he fo entirely won the affection of the king, that he did him the honour to carry him ufually upon his own hand.

Had

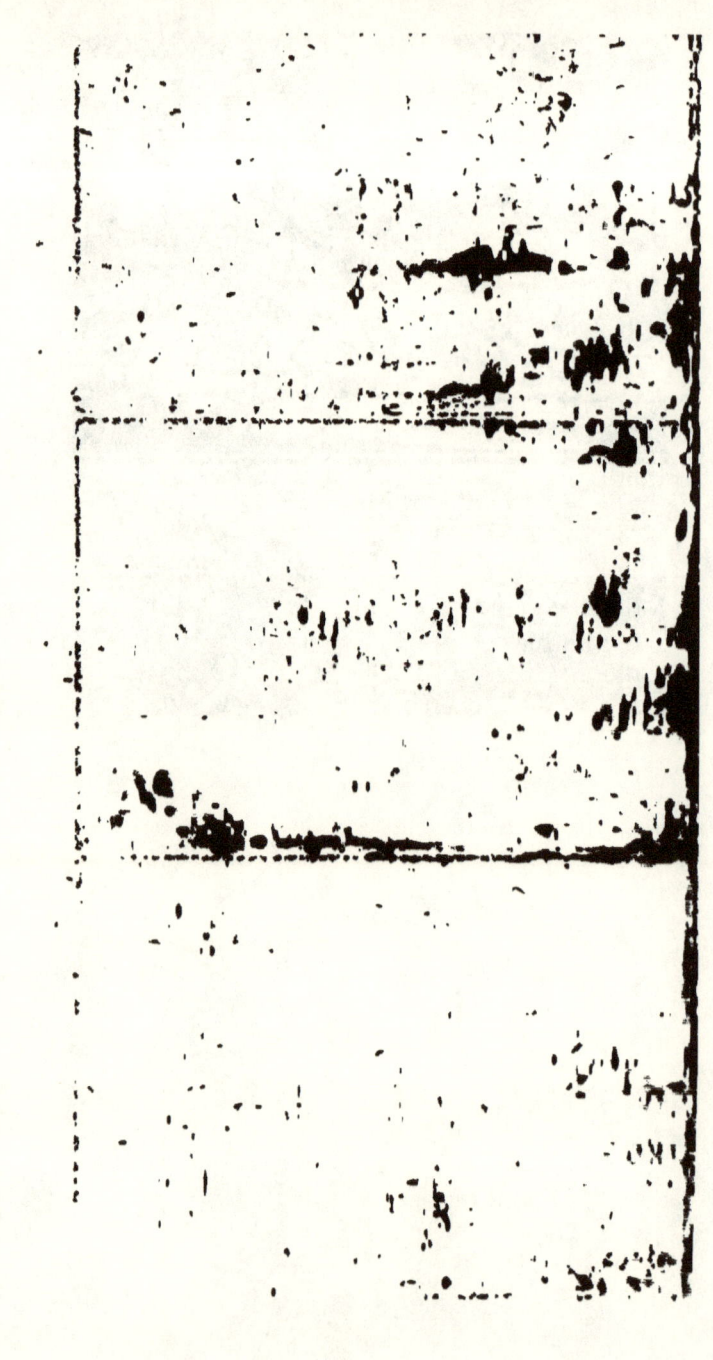

Had he always staid in his nest, concluded the monarch, this good fortune had never befallen him. And you see, by this fable, that it is no unprofitable thing to travel. It rouses the genius of people, and renders them capable of noble atchievements. Dabschelim having ended his discourse; the vizir, after he had made his submissions, and paid his duty according to custom, came forward, and, addressing himself to the king, said, Sir, what your majesty has said is most true; but, I cannot but think yet, that it is not adviseable that a great, a glorious, and a happy, king, should quit his repose for the hardship and danger of travelling. Men of courage, answered the king, delight in labour, fatigue, and danger. If kings, who have power, strip not the thorns from the rose-bushes, the poor can never gather the roses; and, till princes have endured the inconveniences of campaigns, the people can never sleep in peace. Nobody can be safe, in these dominions, while thou seekest nothing but my ease. He that travels meets with rest, and every thing else that he desires, like the leopard, who, by his pains and diligence, and despising the fatigues of travelling, acquired what he wished for. Upon this, the vizir humbly besought the king to relate that fable to his slave; which he did in these words.

C 5    FABLE

## FABLE V.

*The* LEOPARD *and the* LION.

IN the neighbourhood to Bassora, there was a very lovely island, in which grew a most delightful wood, where pleasing breezes whispered their love-stories to the rustling leaves: this enchanting forest was watered with several fountains, whence a number of recreating streams ran gently winding to every part of it. In this lovely place there lodged a leopard, so furious, that even the most daring lions durst not approach within a league of his habitation. For several years his renowned and unequalled courage kept him in peace within this island with a little leopard that was his favourite and heir. To whom said he one day: Son, so soon as thou shalt be strong enough to oppose my enemies, I will resign to thee the care of governing this island, and retire into one corner of it, where I will spend the remainder of my days, without trouble or molestation. But death crossed the old leopard's design: he died when he least dreamt of it, and the young one, before he expected it, succeeded him. The ancient enemies of the old leopard no sooner heard of his death, and the weakness of his successor, but they entered into a league, and together invaded the island; and the young leopard, finding himself unable to withstand such a number of enemies, made his escape into the desarts, and there secured himself. In the mean time his enemies having together made themselves masters of the island, every one

one claimed an equal right to the fovereignty, and each would command in chief. Thus, they fell out, and the bufinefs came to the decifion of a bloody battle, wherein the lion, being victor, drove all the reft of his competitors out of his territories, and became the fole and peaceable mafter of the ifland.

Some years after, the leopard having devoted his life to travel, in one of his journeys meeting an affembled body of lions in a remote part of the foreft, recounted to them his misfortunes, and befought them to affift him in the recovery of his juft inheritance. But the lions, who knew full well the ftrength of the ufurper, refufed their affiftance to the leopard, and replied, Poor filly creature, doft thou not underftand that thy ifland is now under the power of a lion, fo redoubted, that the very birds are afraid to fly over his head? We advife thee rather, added they, to go and wait upon him, fubmiffively offer thy fervices to him, and take fome lucky opportunity privately to revenge the injuries he has done thee. The leopard followed their counfel, went to the lion's court, and there intruding himfelf into the acquaintance of one of the moft favourite domeftics by a thoufand careffes, engaged him to give him an opportunity to difcourfe with his mafter. When he had obtained permiffion, he played his part fo well that the lion found him to be a creature of fo much merit, that he conferred a very noble employment upon him in his court, and in a very little time the leopard fo infinuated himfelf into the lion's favour, that the firft grandees of the court began to grow jealous of him. But their jealoufies were all vain, the lion found him more valuable than them all, and in spite of all their idle malice treated him accordingly. It happened some time after this, that some extraordinary exigence of state called away the lion to a place far distant from the island; but the monarch, being now grown lazy, had no mind to stir out of his delightful abode at a time that the heat was so excessive: this the leopard perceiving, he offered to undertake the voyage himself; and, after he had obtained leave, departed, arrived at the place, dispatched his business, and returned back to court with such an unexpected speed, that the king, admiring his diligence, said to those about him, this leopard is one whom it is impossible for me sufficiently to reward; he contemns labour, and despises hardship, so it be to procure the welfare and peace of my dominions. Having said this, he sent for the leopard, highly applauded his zeal, and, in reward for his services, gave him the government of all his forests, and made him his heir. Now, vizir, had not the leopard undertaken this journey, he had never regained his island.

The minister, now finding that it would be impossible to dissuade the king from the resolution he had taken to travel, said no more to hinder him, and he soon prepared for his journey. During his absence he intrusted those vizirs in whom he had the greatest confidence with the care of his dominions, and charged them, above all things, to be kind and loving to the people. After a thousand admonitions of this kind, and a strict care that none but people worthy their office were left in trust till his return, the glorious Dabschelim, being

being at eafe within himfelf, and in full peace of mind, fet forward with fome of his courtiers for Serandib, where he at length fafely arrived after a long and painful journey. When he had given himfelf the refrefhment of a fhort repofe, he began to think of the bufinefs of his journey. He fpent firft, however, three days in walking about and taking a full view of the city; then leaving his moft cumberfome baggage behind, as alfo fome part of his train, he croffed the mountain, which he found wonderfully high and fteep, but environed with a great number of pleafant gardens and lovely meadows. When he had now croffed the mountain, and was defcending on the other fide, he perceived a very obfcure den, or cavern, which on his enquiry the inhabitants of the mountain told him was the retirement of a certain hermit, called Bidpay, that is to fay, the *friendly phyfician*; and that fome of the Indian grandees called him Pilpay; that he was a perfon of profound knowledge, and had retired from the world in contempt of the hurry and vanity of it, and pleafed himfelf in leading a folitary life. This highly increafed Dabfchelim's curiofity, who therefore went himfelf to the mouth of the cave; and Pilpay, feeing him approach, went out to meet him, and invited him in. The king being entered, the old bramin befought him to reft himfelf, and begged leave to afk him the reafon of his taking fo long and dangerous a journey. The king, who had fomething of a prophetic apprehenfion that he fhould meet with what he fought for in his converfe with this old man, recounted to him the whole ftory of his travels, his dream, the difcovery

covery of the treasure, and what was contained in the piece of white satin. The bramin, then, with a look of the higheft pleafure, told the king he looked upon thofe to be a happy people who lived under his reign, and that he could not sufficiently applaud his having contemned the fatigues of a tedious journey to acquire knowledge for the felicity of his fubjects. Then, taking occafion hence, he opened his lips, like a cabinet of precious knowledge, and charmed Dabfchelim with his admirable difcourfes. After feveral other things, they talked concerning Houfchenk's letter. Dabfchelim read the admonitions which it contained one after the other: At the end of each, Pilpay gave the fables which ferved to illuftrate them, and the monarch heedfully kept them in his memory.

CHAP.

## CHAP. II.

*That we ought to avoid the infinuations of* FLATTERERS *and* BACK-BITERS.

THE first admonition, said the monarch to the bramin, contained in this most inestimable legacy of moral precepts, is, *That kings ought never to listen to false reports, or the insinuating malice of flatterers, which never produce any thing but misfortunes, and always bring an ill end to such as hearken to them.* Whoever, cried the bramin, observes not this command, must needs be ignorant of the fable of the *Lion and the Ox*. Upon which, the king being desirous to hear it, Pilpay in the following manner began the fables.

---

### FABLE I.

*The* MERCHANT *and his* LEWD CHILDREN; *being the introduction to the Fable of the* LION *and the* OX.

A Certain merchant, a man well skilled in the affairs of the world, falling sick, and perceiving that his age and his distemper would not long

long permit him to live, called his three sons together, who were very debauched, and wasted his estate in riot and disorder. Sons, said he, I know you may be in some measure excused for thus consuming my estate, inasmuch as that ye know not what it costs to get it: but it becomes you to learn, at least, that riches should be only properly made instrumental to acquire the blessings of heaven and earth. There are three things that men of different tempers and dispositions labour for in this world with more than ordinary vehemence. The first is, to enjoy all the pleasures of life; and the seekers after these are the people who are addicted to intemperance, and abandon themselves to sensual delights. The second is, to obtain high dignities and preferments: those who endeavour after these are the ambitious, who only love to command and be admired. The third is, to acquire more valuable and more lasting joys, the joys of heaven; and to take delight in doing good to others. Those, who place their happiness in these noble enjoyments, deserve the highest admiration and applauses. - But, my sons, there is no way to attain the last great end, but by the means of wealth well got. Now, seeing that what we seek for in this world is not to be had without money, *that*, as it can procure us whatever we search for, must be first of all acquired, and most carefully preserved: but they, who meet an estate already got to their hands, know not the trouble of getting it, and that is the reason they consume it so prodigally. Therefore, dear children, give over this irregular life, take care of yourselves, and rather endeavour to increase your estates than to waste them in these idle extravagances. Father,

ther, replied the eldeſt ſon, you command us to acquire, but you ſhould conſider that acquiſition depends only upon fortune. This alſo I am perfectly convinced of, that we ſhall never want what is deſtined us, though we ſhould never ſtir a foot to obtain it: on the other ſide, we ſhall never be maſters of what is not ordained for us, though we ſhould torment ourſelves to death in the endeavouring after it. I remember an old proverb: *Whenever I fled what deſtiny had allotted, I always met with it; but, whenever I ſought for that which never was appointed me, I never could find it.* This is clearly to be ſeen by the fable of the old king's two ſons; of which one diſcovered his father's treaſures, and gained the kingdom with little trouble, while the other loſt it, though he did all he could to preſerve it. The father on this deſired that he might hear this ſtory, which his ſon rehearſed as follows.

## FABLE II.
### The KING and his TWO SONS.

IN the country of Ardos\* there lived an ancient king who had two ſons, both covetous, yet given to debauchery. This monarch, finding the infirmities of age increaſe upon him, and that he was haſting to the other world, and conſidering the humour of his two ſons, was much afraid that after his death they would diſſipate in idle expence the vaſt treaſure which he had heaped together, and therefore reſolved to hide it. With this deſign he went to a religious hermit, who had

---
\*Ardos is a province to the north-eaſt of the river Indus.

retired

retired from the world, and in whom he had a very great confidence. By the counsel of this hermit, the treasure was buried in the earth near where the hermit dwelt, so privately that nobody knew any thing of it. This done, the king made his will, which he put into the hermit's hands, with these farther orders. I charge you, said he, yet to reveal this treasure to my children when after my death you see them in the distresses of poverty. It may be, added the king, that, when they have suffered a little hardship, they will become more prudent in their conduct.

The hermit having promised all fidelity in the observance of the king's commands, the monarch returned to his palace, and, in a short time after, died; nor did the hermit long survive him: the treasure therefore lay concealed, probably for ever to continue so, in the hermitage. The king being now dead, the sons could not agree about the succession. This occasioned a bloody war between them; and the eldest, who was the more powerful, utterly despoiled his younger brother of all that he had. This young prince, thus deprived of his inheritance, fell into a deep melancholy, and resolved to quit the world. To that purpose he left the city, and calling to mind the kindness between his father and the hermit, There is no other way for me, said he to himself, but to find out this honest man, that I may learn of him to live as he does, and end my life in peace and contentedness in his company. With this resolution he left the city, but, coming to the hermitage, found that the hermit was dead. He was greatly afflicted and disappointed at this unexpected chance; but at length came

to

to a refolution to live as he had done, and accordingly made choice of his retirement for his habitation.

Now there was in this hermitage a well, which had been ufed to fupply the place with water, but it was now dry; to enquire into the caufe of this, the unhappy prince ventured to let himfelf down to the bottom of the well: but how great was his aftonifhment! when he faw the lower part of it for a great depth filled with his father's treafures. On finding this he was thankful to heaven, and wifely took up a refolution to lay out his money with more moderation than he had done before.

On the other hand, his brother, who fat fecurely revelling upon his throne without the care of his people or his army, imagining with himfelf that his father's treafure was hid in the palace, as he told him upon his death-bed, one day, being at war with a neighbouring prince, was obliged to have recourfe to his expected treafure. But how was he amazed, after he had fought a long time and found nothing. This quite difabled him from raifing a powerful army, and threw him into a very great fit of melancholy. However, making a virtue of neceffity, he raifed what force he could, and marched out of the city to meet and encounter his enemy. The battle was obftinate, and this king and his enemy were both flain; fo that the two armies enraged at the lofs of their leaders, fell to butcher each other with equal fury, till at length the generals, having agreed together that it would be their better way to choofe a mild and gentle king for the government of the ftate, went and found
out.

out the young prince, who was retired to the hermitage, conducted him in great pomp to the royal palace, and set him upon the throne.

This fable shews, that it is better for men to rely upon providence than to torment themselves about the acquisition of a thing that was never ordained them. When the young man had ended his fable, all this, said the father, may be true; but all effects have their causes, and he, who relies upon providence without considering these, had need to be instructed by the ensuing fable.

## FABLE III.
### The DERVISE, the FALCON, and the RAVEN.

A Certain dervise used to relate, that in his youth, once passing through a wood, and admiring the works of the great Author of nature, he spied a falcon that held a piece of flesh in his beak; and, hovering about a tree, tore the flesh into bits, and gave it to a young raven that lay bald and featherless in its nest. The dervise, admiring the bounty of providence, in a rapture of admiration cried out, Behold this poor bird, that is not able to seek out sustenance for itself, is not however forsaken of its Creator, who spreads the whole world like a table, where all creatures have their food ready provided for them. He extends his liberality so far, that the serpent finds wherewith to live upon the mountain of Gahen*. Why then am I so greedy, and wherefore

---

* A mountain in the east, famous for a vast number of venomous animals.

do

do I run to the ends of the earth, and plow up the ocean for bread? Is it not better that I should henceforward confine myself in repose to some little corner, and abandon myself to fortune. Upon this he retired to his cell, where, without putting himself to any farther trouble for any thing in this world, he remained three days and three nights without victuals. At last, Servant of mine, said the Creator to him in a dream, know thou that all things in this world have their causes: and, though my providence can never be limited, my wisdom requires that men shall make use of the means that I have ordained them. If thou wouldst imitate any one of the birds thou hast seen to my glory, use the talents I have given thee, and imitate the falcon that feeds the raven, and not the raven that lies a sluggard in his nest, and expects his food from another.

This example shews us, that we are not to lead idle and lazy lives upon the pretence of depending on providence. On this, the elder son was silenced, but the second son, taking upon him to speak, said to his father, you advise us, sir, to labour, and get estates and riches, but, when we have heaped up a great deal of wealth, is it not also necessary that you inform us what we shall do with it? It is easy to acquire wealth, replied the father, but a difficult thing to expend it well. Riches many times prove very fatal; an instance of which you may see in the following fable.

FABLE

## FABLE IV.

*The* COUNTRYMAN *and several* RATS.

THERE was once a certain husbandman, who had a barn full of corn, which he carefully kept close locked up; not far from this lived a rat, who long laboured on every side of it, endeavouring to make a hole somewhere to creep in at. After great trouble he at length found his way into the barn; where when he had thoroughly filled his belly, amazed at the vast treasures which he saw himself master of, away he ran, full of joy, and gave notice of it to a multitude of other rats, his neighbours, telling them of his immense riches, but carefully concealing the place where they lay. On the news of his good fortune, all the rats of the neighbouring villages presently flocked about him, and made him a thousand offers of their service, scraping and cringing to him, and soothing him in all the excursions of his fantastic humour. The fool, taking all this for reality, grew very proud and stately, as believing himself to be some extraordinary person; and, never considering that this magazine was not to last always, began most extravagantly to play the prodigal at the poor husbandman's cost, treating his companions and flatterers every day with as much as they could cram down. At this juncture of time, there happened in the same country so terrible a famine, that the poor cried out for bread while the rat lay wallowing in plenty. The husbandman, now believing it his time to make the best of his corn,

corn, opened his barn-door; but, finding a moſt unexpected conſumption of his ſtore, he fell into a paſſion, and preſently removed what he had to another place. The rat, who looked upon himſelf to be ſole maſter of miſ-rule in the barn, was then aſleep, but his paraſites were awake; and, ſeeing the huſbandman go and come, ſoon began to fear there was ſomething the matter, and that they ſhould by and by be murdered for their monſtrous robberies. Upon this they betook themſelves every one to flight, leaving the poor cullied rat faſt aſleep, not one of them having gratitude enough to give him the leaſt hint of the danger that threatened him. This is the practice of your ſmell-feaſt friends: while you keep a plentiful table they are your moſt humble and obedient ſervants; but, when the accommodation fails, like Tartars, they ſeek for other paſtures, and leave you to deſtruction.

The rat, however, ſoon after waking, was amazed to find none of his pick-thanks at his elbow; he left his hole in great haſte to know the cauſe, which he too ſoon found out; for, going to the barn and finding all was gone, not ſo much being left as would ſuffice him for that day, he fell into ſuch a deep deſpair, that in anger and diſtraction he beat out his brains againſt the next wall, and ſo ended his days. This example, ſon, ſhews us that we ought to live according to our income.

The ſecond brother being ſilenced alſo by this ſtory, the youngeſt, taking his turn, ſaid, Father, you have well inſtructed us how to gain money, and to guard againſt the fooliſh waſting it; but now pray inform us, when we have acquired this

wealth

corn, opened his barn-door; but, finding a moſt unexpected confumption of his ſtore, he fell into a paſſion, and prefently removed what he had to another place. The rat, who looked upon himſelf to be fole maſter of mif-rule in the barn, was then aſleep, but his paraſites were awake; and, feeing the huſbandman go and come, foon began to fear there was ſomething the matter, and that they ſhould by and by be murdered for their monſtrous robberies. Upon this they betook themſelves every one to flight, leaving the poor cullied rat faſt aſleep, not one of them having gratitude enough to give him the leaſt hint of the danger that threatened him. This is the practice of your ſmell-feaſt friends: while you keep a plentiful table they are your moſt humble and obedient ſervants; but, when the accommodation fails, like Tartars, they feek for other paſtures, and leave you to deſtruction.

The rat, however, foon after waking, was amazed to find none of his pick-thanks at his elbow; he left his hole in great haſte to know the cauſe, which he too foon found out; for, going to the barn and finding all was gone, not ſo much being left as would ſuffice him for that day, he fell into ſuch a deep deſpair, that in anger and diſtraction he beat out his brains againſt the next wall, and ſo ended his days. This example, fon, ſhews us that we ought to live according to our income.

The ſecond brother being ſilenced alfo by this ſtory, the youngeſt, taking his turn, said, Father, you have well inſtructed us how to gain money, and to guard againſt the fooliſh waſting it; but now pray inform us, when we have acquired this

wealth

wealth you speak of, what is to be done with it? It is to be made use of, replied the father, upon all just occasions; but more especially for the conveniences of life, according to the rules of temperance and justice. In the first place, your expences ought not to be such as afterwards to be repented of by yourselves, or condemned by others as the waste of prodigality: and, in the second, it is a good general rule against the other extreme, that no man ought by his avarice to render himself hateful to the world.

The father having thus exhorted his children to follow his counsel, they betook themselves all three to particular callings: The eldest of them turned merchant, and travelled into foreign countries: among other goods, which he purchased for the sake of trade, he had two oxen; both the calves of the same cow, and both very fair and beautiful; the one was called Cohotorbe, and the other Mandebe. Our merchant took great care to feed up these oxen; but, because his journey was long, they, in spite of their good feeding, before they arrived at the end of it, grew to be weak and lean. While they were in this poor condition, they met with a quagmire on the road, into which Cohotorbe fell, and stuck so fast, that the merchant had much ado to get him out again; and, even when he had got him out, he found the poor beast was so weak, that, being hardly able to stand, he was forced to leave him behind with another man, till he could recover strength to continue his journey: this man, after he had kept him three days in the desart, grew weary of his charge, left Cohotorbe to feed by himself, and sent the merchant word that his ox was dead.

dead. In a little time after, Mandebe died of over-fatigue; and Cohotorbe, having now a little recovered his flesh, began to enjoy his liberty, and ramble from one place to another; and, coming at length into a meadow that pleased him very well, stayed there for some time, living in ease and plenty; so that he became, in a little more time, as fair and plump as ever he was before.

Not far from this meadow there dwelt, unknown to Cohotorbe, a lion, who made all the inhabitants of the woods round about him tremble, and commanded over several other lions, who believed him to be the most potent sovereign in the world. This powerful monarch of the beasts, near whom nothing of the beef-kind had ever ventured to approach, when he heard the bellowing of our ox, which was a noise he had never heard before, was seized with extreme terror, and no motive could fetch him from his den to face this unknown enemy. Ashamed, however, to discover his fears to his courtiers, he pretended an illness that made him unable to stir out of his palace. This king of the woods, among the rest of his domestic servants, had two foxes that were as cunning as two crocodiles, one of which was called Kalila, and the other Damna; these were both beasts of great intrigue; but the latter, which was the male, was more proud and more ambitious than the former. One day, says this inquisitive fox to his wife, Pr'ythee, deary, what is it, thinkest thou, ails the king, that he dares not walk abroad as he used to do? To whom Kalila answered, Pr'ythee, dear, let us never trouble ourselves about these matters; it is sufficient for you and me to live peaceably under his protection without examining what he does. It is not for us to prate about state-affairs; and let me tell you, spouse, they, that meddle with things that no way concern them, are in danger of the same misfortune that befel the ape. And pray, replied the husband, what was that? To whom the female fox made this reply.

---

## FABLE V.

### The CARPENTER and the APE.

AN ape, one day, sat staring upon a carpenter who was cleaving a piece of wood with two wedges, which he put into the cleft one after another, as the split opened. The carpenter soon after getting away to his dinner, and leaving his work half done, the ape would needs turn log-cleaver; and, coming to the piece of wood, pulled out one wedge without putting in the other; so that the wood, having nothing to keep it asunder, closed immediately again, and, catching the meddling fool fast by the two fore feet, there held him till the surly carpenter returned, who, without ceremony, knocked him on the head for meddling with his work.

This fable, spouse, instructs us, that we ought not to meddle with other people's business. Ah, replied Damna, but these are but foolish stories; and let me tell you, it is not for those that serve kings to be idle: they must be always endeavouring to advance themselves. Know you not the fable of the two companions, one of which,

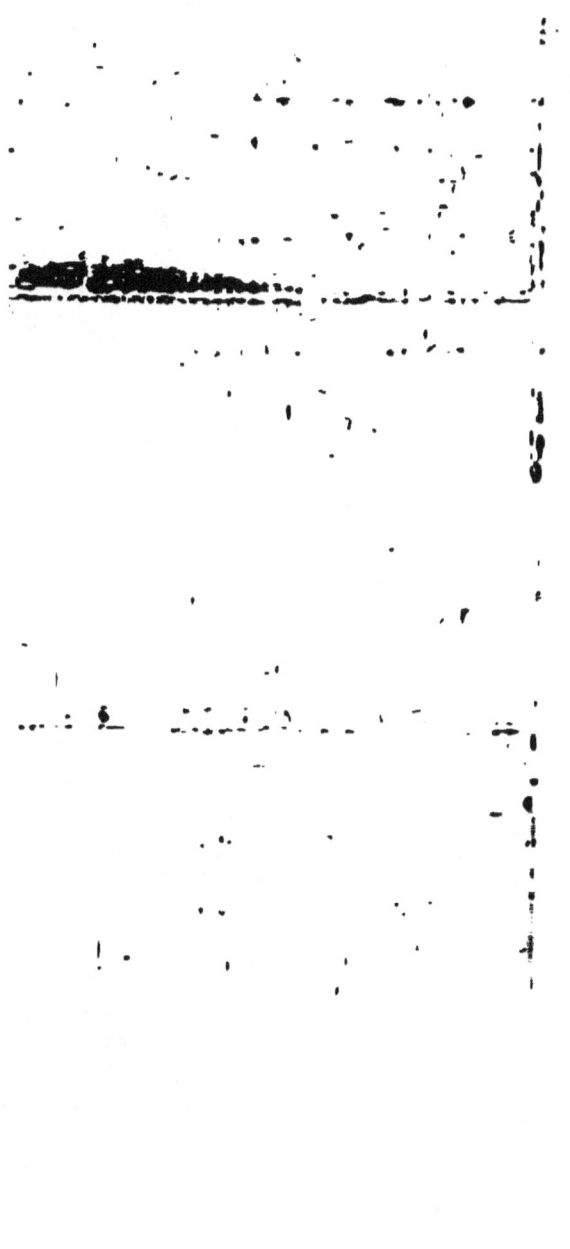

which, by his industry, obtained a crown; while the other, being slothful and faint-hearted, fell into extreme misery?

## FABLE VI.

### The two TRAVELLERS.

THERE were once two friends, who made a resolution never to leave each other. In pursuance of this, for a long time, they always travelled together. But, one day, as they were journeying in search of their common advantages, they came to a deep river at the foot of a hill; and the place was so delightful, that they resolved to rest themselves by the stream. After they were well refreshed, they began to look about them, and please their eyes with what they could discover most curious in so pleasant a place; and at length cast their eyes upon a white stone, that contained the following words written in blue letters.

Travellers, we have prepared an excellent banquet for your welcome; but you must be bold, and deserve it before you can obtain it: what you are to do is this: Throw yourself boldly into this fountain, and swim to the other side; you shall there meet with a lion carved in white stone; this you must take upon your shoulders, and, without stopping, run with it to the top of yonder mountain, never fearing the wild beasts that surround you, nor the thorns that prick your feet; for, be assured nothing will hurt you: and, as soon as you get to the top of the hill, you will

will immediately find yourselves in possession of great felicity: but, if you cease going forward, you shall never come to the happiness; nor shall the slothful ever attain to what is here prepared for the industrious.

Then Ganem, for that was the name of one of the two companions, says to Salem, for so was the other called, Brother, here are means prescribed us that will put an end to all our pains and travel; let us take courage, and try whether what this stone contains be true or false. Dear brother, replied Salem, it is not for a man of sense to give credit to such an idle writing as this appears to me to be; and, in a vain expectation of I know not what uncertain gain, to throw himself into evident danger. Friend, replied Ganem, they who have courage contemn danger to make themselves happy; there is no gathering the rose without being pricked by the thorns. Be that as it will, answered Salem, it is but romantic valour that prompts us to attempt enterprizes, the end of which we know not, even though we should succeed; and, if we are in our senses, we must see that it is not our business, for the sake of a dark promise, to throw ourselves into this water, that seems to be a kind of an abyss, whence it may not be so easy to get out again. A rational man, brother, never moves one of his feet till the other be fixed. Perhaps this writing may be a mere whimsy, the idle diversion of some wandering beggar; or, even if it should be real, perhaps when you have cross'd this river, this lion of stone may prove so heavy, that you may not be able to do as you are ordered, and run with it, without stopping, to the top of the mountain. But, suppofing even that all this were eafy for you to perform, yet, truft me, it is not worth while to attempt it; for, when you have done whatever is by you to be done, you know not what will be the iffue of your trouble. For my part I will be no fharer with you in dangers of this kind, but fhall ufe all my rhetoric to endeavour to diffuade you from fuch idle and chimerical undertakings. No perfuafions, replied Ganem, fhall make me alter my refolution; and therefore, if you will not follow me, dear friend, at leaft be pleafed to fee me venture. Salem, feeing him fo refolute, cried out, deareft brother, if you are weak enough, in your reafon, to determine on this rafh, and to me diftracted, undertaking, give me a laft embrace, and farewel for ever; you have refufed my admonitions, and I have not the power to ftay and be a witnefs of your ruin. On this they took a parting embrace; and Salem, taking his leave of his, as he fuppofed, unhappy brother, fet forward upon his journey.

On the other hand, Ganem went to the brink of the river, refolving to perifh or to win the prize. He found it deep, but, ftrengthened by his courage, he threw himfelf in, and fwam to the other fide. When he had recovered the dry land, he refted himfelf a while; and then, lifting up the lion, which he faw before him, with all his might ran with it, without ftopping, to the top of the mountain. When he had reached the top, he had before him the profpect of a very fair and glorious city, which, as he was attentively viewing, there iffued from the lion of ftone, fuch a terrible thundering noife, that the mountain,

tain, and all the places round about it, trembled. This noise no sooner reached the ears of the inhabitants of the city, but they came running up to Ganem, who was not a little astonished to see them; and presently some, that seemed to be superior to the rest in quality and degree, accosted him with great respect and ceremony; and, after they had harangued him with many large encomiums, they set him upon a horse sumptuously caparisoned, conducted him to the city, where they made him put on the royal robes, and proclaimed him king of all the country. When this ceremony was over, and the inhabitants seemed all very well pleased with their king, the new monarch desired to understand the reason of his advancement: to which they answered, that the learned men of the kingdom had, in regard to the future happiness of their country, by virtue of a talisman, so charmed the fountain which he had crossed, and the lion of stone which he carried to the top of the mountain, that, whenever their king died, any one, who was so adventurous as to expose himself to the hazards he had done, and brought the lion safe to the top of the mountain, had this reward for his courage; that the lion roared out so prodigiously, that the inhatants, hearing the noise, might go forth in search of the person who had arrived with it, to make him their king. This custom, pursued they, has been of long continuance, and was meant to ensure us, for our king, a man of courage and resolution; and, since the lot has fallen upon your majesty, your sovereignty is absolute among us.

I

I have rehearsed this fable to you, spouse, continued the male-fox, to let you understand, that there is no tasting pleasure without trouble. But, as courage and resolution you see are the sure ways to preferment, I have resolved never to give over till I am one of the greatest lords in the court. Kalila asked her spouse, on this, what means he intended to make use of to attain his ends; why you see, answered Damna, that our sovereign lord the lion seems to be seized with astonishment, and great uneasiness; now, I have determined to attempt, at least, to cure him of his disquiet. How canst thou presume, cried Kalila, to give counsel to a king, that never wert accustomed to the cabals of princes? Persons of wit, replied Damna, never want either the means or industry to accomplish their designs. I remember that, one day, a handicraft tradesman, who, by his industry and genius, had gained a kingdom, received a letter from a neighbouring prince, wherein he expostulated with the new king after this manner: *Thou, that didst never handle before any other than a chizzel or a saw, how darest thou presume to govern a kingdom?* To which the carpenter returned for answer, he, that gave me wit enough to guide a saw, will also give me judgement to wield a sword; with which, I doubt not, but I shall be able to chastise the insolence of any of my too arrogant neighbours. I know very well, replied Kalila, my dear, that you have both genius and courage; but let me put you in mind, that kings do not always cherish, with their favours, those who have wit and merit to deserve them; but their oldest servants, and such as have done the state important service, generally are the people who have the greatest share of their favours; and, as you are but a new comer, and indeed none of the most eminent of the king's servants, when you consider this, (which, believe me, is the true state of the case,) what can you pretend to? Value me not, replied Damna, on the merit of what I am at court at present; for, let me tell you, I hope, in a short time, to have a much more considerable employment. I well know what are the methods of ingratiating one's self with great persons, and let me, for your own sake, inform you, that they, who aspire to be admitted into the cabinets of princes, ought to have five particular qualifications: Which are, *never to be in a passion; to avoid pride; not to be covetous; to be sincere; and never to be astonished at the changes of fortune.* These are very good maxims, replied Kalila, in all states of life; but, pray, tell me, supposing you were advanced to be the king's favourite, what are the virtues you would practise to keep his esteem? I would serve him, replied Damna, with a perfect fidelity; I would punctually obey him; and, whatever the king does, always believe his intentions good: I would persuade him to do good, by laying before him the benefit he will receive thereby, and dissuade him from doing whatever may be prejudicial to himself or his kingdom. I find, said Kalila, thou hast resolved to go on with this design, and must needs own thou seemest to have well qualified thyself for it; but yet let me warn thee to have a care what thou dost; for, it is a dangerous thing to serve a prince. Wise men say, that *there are three sorts of per-*

*sons*

*sons who are wholly deprived of judgement; they who are ambitious of preferments in the courts of princes; they who make use of poison, to shew their skill in curing it; and they who entrust women with their secrets.* A king is well compared to a high mountain, upon which there are mines of precious stones, and also numerous herds of wild devouring beasts: it is a difficult thing to a :ost these, but more dangerous to inhabit them. Kings are also well compared to a wide ocean, wherein sea-faring people generally either make their fortunes, or perish. I am not ignorant of all this, replied Damna in his turn, but know also that kings resemble fire, which will burn those that approach too near it; but let me also tell thee, wife, that he, who is afraid to adventure, will never come to any thing. After this discourse, Damna went to wait upon the lion, and, as soon as he approached his presence, made him a profound reverence. The lion took immediate notice of him, and asked who he was. To which some of his courtiers replied, that he was such an one, and that his father had a long time served his majesty. Oh, said the king, I now remember him.—Then turning to Damna, Well friend, said the monarch very graciously, where do you live?——I supply my father's place in your majesty's household, replied Damna, but till now I never durst presume to appear in your majesty's presence with the offer of my service. I hope your majesty will not disdain the oblation of my faithful intentions, though I am the meanest and unworthiest of your majesty's servants: dry wood is, sometimes, as much esteemed as a beautiful tree. The lion was much pleased with

Damna's eloquence, and, looking upon his courtiers, Wit, said he, resembles fire, which will shew itself though covered with ashes. Damna was so overjoyed that his compliment had pleased the king, that he took his opportunity to beg a private audience of his majesty; and, when they were together; Sir, said Damna, first let me implore your majesty's pardon for presuming to speak before your majesty; and then, if I may presume so far, beseech your majesty to let me know the cause of your melancholy retirement; for, within these few days, I have, with great sorrow, observed your majesty has not been so chearful as you were wont to be. Fain would the lion have concealed his fear; but, pleased with Damna's winning behaviour, and wanting some one to unbosom his grief to, he determined to entrust him with the fatal secret of his fears. Just as he was about to utter the cause of his troubles, behold Cohotorbe set up a most terrible bellowing; this so disordered his countenance, that he found himself constrained, even though he had not before intended it, to tell Damna, that the terrible noise of this beast, whatever he was, was the cause of all his disturbance. I imagine, said the king, that the body of the beast, which I hear bellow so dreadfully, must be proportionable to the sound of his voice; and that, being so, it is in vain for us to think of resisting him, and, indeed, it is little better than madness for us to tarry any longer in these woods. Is this all that troubles your majesty, said Damna? Nothing else, answered the lion, and this I think sufficient. Sir, replied Damna, you ought not to quit your princely habitation for this: it is not for a king to be afraid of of a meer found, but rather to fortify his courage with so much the greater resolution. Those creatures that make the loudest noises are not always the biggest nor the strongest. A crane, as big as he is, has neither strength nor courage to encounter the smallest hawk: and he, that suffers himself to be deluded by bulk of body, may likely enough be deceived as the fox was.

## FABLE VII.

### The Fox and the Hen.

THERE was once, continued Damna, a certain fox, who, eagerly searching about for something to appease his hunger, at length spied a hen that was busily scratching the earth and picking up worms at the foot of a tree. Upon the same tree there also hung a drum, which made a noise every now and then, the branches being moved by the violence of the wind, and beating upon it. The fox was just going to fling himself upon the hen, and make amends for a long fast, when he first heard the noise of the drum. Oh ho, quoth he, looking up, are you there, I will be with you by and by; that body, whatever it be, I promise myself must certainly have more flesh upon it than a sorry hen; so saying, he clambered up the tree, and in the mean while the hen made her escape. The greedy and famished fox seized his prey, and fell to work with teeth and claws upon it. But, when he had torn off the head of the drum, and found there was nothing within but an empty cavity,

cavity,—air inſtead of fleſh and griſtles, and a meer hollowneſs inſtead of good guts and garbage,—fetching a deep ſigh; Unfortunate wretch that I am, cried he, what a delicate morſel have I loſt, only for the ſhow of a large bellyful!

I have recited this example, concluded he, to the end your majeſty may not be terrified with the ſound of the bellowing noiſe you hear, becauſe loud and ſtrenuous, for, there is no certainty from that of its coming from a terrible beaſt; and if you pleaſe I will go and ſee what ſort of creature it is. To which the lion conſented; nevertheleſs, when Damna was gone, he repented his having ſent him. For, ſaid the monarch to himſelf, I ſhould have remembered my father's excellent rule, that it is a great error in a prince to diſcover his ſecrets to any, but eſpecially that there are ten ſorts of people who are never to be entruſted with them. Theſe are, 1. Thoſe whom he has uſed ill without a cauſe. 2. Thoſe who have loſt their eſtates or their honour at court. 3. Thoſe who have been degraded from their employments without any hopes of ever being reſtored to them again. 4. Thoſe that love nothing but ſedition and diſturbance. 5. Thoſe that ſee their kindred or acquaintance in preferments whence themſelves have been excluded. 6. Such as having committed any crime have been more ſeverely puniſhed than others who have tranſgreſſed in the ſame manner. 7. Such as have done good ſervice, and have been but ill rewarded for it. 8. Enemies reconciled by conſtraint. 9. Thoſe who believe the ruin of the prince will turn to
their

their advantage. 10. and laftly, Thofe who believe themfelves lefs obliged to their fovereign than to his enemy. And, as thefe are together fo numerous a clafs of perfons, I wifh I have not done imprudently in difcovering my fecrets to Damna.

While the king was making thefe reflections to himfelf, Damna returned, and told him, with a fmiling countenance, that the beaft which made fuch a noife was no other than an ox, that was feeding in a meadow without any other defign than to fpend his days lazily in eating and fleeping. And, added Damna, if your majefty thinks it convenient, I will fo order the matter, that he fhall be glad to come and enrol himfelf in the number of your fervants. The lion was extremely pleafed with Damna's propofals, and made him a fign to go and fetch the ox into his prefence. On this, Damna went immediately to Cohotorbe, and afked him whence he came, and what accident had brought him into thofe quarters? In anfwer to which, when Cohotorbe had related his hiftory at large, Damna faid, friend, I am very glad I have happened to fee thee, for, it may be in my power to do thee a fingular fervice, by acquainting thee with the ftate of the place thou haft accidentally wandered into. Know, then, that here lives a lion not far off, who is the king of all the beafts of this country, and that he is, though a terrible enemy, yet a moft kind and tender friend to all the beafts who put themfelves under his protection. When I firft faw you here, I acquainted his majefty with it, and he has gracioufly defired to fee thee, and given me orders to conduct you to his palace. If thou wilt follow me, I promife thee the favour

of

of being admitted into his service and protection; but, if thou refusest to go along with me, know that thou hast not many days to live in this place. So soon as the ox but heard the word *lion* pronounced, he trembled for fear; but, recovering himself a little as Damna continued his speech, he at length made answer, If thou wilt assure me that he shall do me no harm I will follow thee. Damna, on this, immediately swore to him; and Cohotorbe, upon the faith of his oaths, consented to go and wait upon the lion. Damna, on this, ran before to give the king notice of Cohotorbe's coming; and our ox, arriving soon after, made a profound reverence to the king, who received him with great kindness, and asked him what occasion had brought him into his dominions? In answer to which, when the ox had recounted to him all his adventures, Remain here, said the lion, with us, and live in peace; for I permit all my subjects to live within my dominions in repose and tranquillity. The ox, having returned his majesty thanks for his kind reception, promised to serve him with a real fidelity; and at length insinuated himself in such a manner into the lion's favour, that he gained his majesty's confidence, and became his most intimate favourite.

This, however, was matter of great affliction to poor Damna, who, when he saw that Cohotorbe was in greater esteem at court than himself, and that he was the only depository of the king's secrets, it wrought in him so desperate a jealousy, that he could not rest, but was ready to hang himself with vexation. In the fulness of his heart he flew to make his moan to Kalila.

Kalila. O my dear wife, said he, I have taken a world of care and pains to gain the king's favour, and all to no purpose: I brought, you may remember, into his presence the object that occasioned all his disturbances, and that very ox is now become the sole cause of my disquiet. To which Kalila answered, Spouse, you ought not to complain of what you have done, or at least you have nobody to blame but yourself. You should have considered that this might prove the consequence, when you undertook this enterprize, for you are now just in the condition of the dervise who left his habitation.

## FABLE VIII.

*The* DERVISE *that left his Habitation.*

A Certain king once presented a dervise, who was a great favourite with him, with a very rich habit; of which a cunning thief, in the neighbourhood, having notice, made use of the following stratagem to cheat him of it. He went, with a down-cast look and demure countenance, to the dervise in his habitation, and pretended an earnest desire to serve him, and that the utmost of his ambition was to attend on him as his master, and great example in holiness, as long as he lived. The dervise, overjoyed that he had got a novice who seemed to be so piously inclined, most willingly received him; but the thief, taking the first opportunity, stole the habit and carried it away. The dervise, missing at once both his rich clothes and his novice, mistrusted the business;

business; and so, leaving his habitation, resolved to go to the city in search of the robber. As he travelled upon the road, he met with two rams that were very furiously encountering one another, and interchanged such desperate horn-blows, that the blood ran down on every side. A fox, who was a witness of the combat, made his own advantage of it, and licked up the blood: but at length, as he was licking, he received such a terrible blow over the head from one of the rams, that he died on the spot.

The dervise stopt a good while to behold, and moralise upon, this accident, and, in short, stayed so long, that, when he came to the city, the gates were shut. A good-natured woman, however, that lived in the city, looking out at window, and perceiving he wanted a lodging, called to him, and offered him the conveniency of her house. The dervise, who was honest himself, and therefore suspected no harm of others, very readily accepted her kindness, went into the house, and, as soon as he was entered, thrust himself into a corner to say his usual prayers. This woman, as the devil would have it, was a bawd, and kept a bevy of pretty girls, whose favours she sold to the young gentry of the place. Now among these girls there was one who was so violently beloved by a young gentleman, and of whom he was so jealous, that he would admit nobody else to come near her; which they, who were enamoured of her as well as himself, took so ill, that they persuaded the young girl to rid herself of his company. And the girl, who feared him more than she loved him, listening to the persuasions of her other lovers, made her jealous

tyrant

tyrant drunk, and the fame night blew a poifonous powder up into his noſtrils: this powder, however, as miſchief often rebounds on thoſe who occaſion it, forcing the young man to ſneeze, the ſtrength of the ſternutation blew a part of it into the courtezan's mouth; and ſhe, not being able to prevent its going down her throat, felt the effects of her own poiſon, and died the ſame hour. The poor derviſe, who was a trembling witneſs to all this, was aſtoniſhed at the monſtrous wickedneſs of the world, and thought the night extremely long.

As ſoon as day came, he made haſte to leave ſo dangerous a place, and took a lodging at a ſhoemaker's houſe, who received him with open arms. The ſame evening, however, the hoſt, being invited to a feaſt from which it was impoſſible for him to abſent himſelf, recommended to his family the care and good uſage of his gueſt.

Now this ſhoemaker's wife had a gallant, whom ſhe was extremely fond of; he was handſome, well-made, a man of ſome wit, and good-humoured; this loving couple met frequently together by means of a certain old ſurgeon's wife, who was ſo cunning a ſolicitreſs of lechery, that ſhe could have reconciled fire and water into an amorous conjunction; and had her tongue ſo well hung, and was ſo perfect in the art of wheedling, that ſhe would have made you believe a ſtone was made of wax. Whenever the ſhoemaker's wife knew her huſband was ſafe abroad, ſhe made uſe of this miſtreſs *Go-between*, to give notice to her paramour of his abſence; and now, believing ſhe had an excellent

cellent opportunity, sent her away forthwith to tell her gallant the good news. Away comes he upon the first intimation: but, by what ill luck I know not, as he was knocking at the door, the shoemaker arrived, and finding the man, whom he already suspected to be the grafter of his forehead, had had such good intelligence, in he went, and, without saying a word, beat his wife, tied her to a post, and so went to bed.

While the moody cuckold, who had tired his arms with bestowing his strap upon his wife, was fast asleep, and dreaming, I warrant, of rams, stags, oxen, and other horned beasts, in comes the pious *Go-between*, the surgeon's wife, and not knowing any thing of what had happened, and having found out the shoemaker's wife in the dark, 'Slife, sister, says she, why do you let the young man stay so long at the door! for shame, go and fetch him in. To whom the disappointed bondwoman answered, with a deep sigh and a low voice, I believe, says she, some malicious demon or other sent my husband back from supper; for, home he came in such a rage, that, not satisfied with almost breaking my bones, he has here tied me to a post. Now, if you would do a charitable act, unbind me, and stand in my place a moment, while I go and beg pardon of my dear friend for having made him stay so long; which done, I will immediately come back and be tied as I was.

The surgeon's wife, moved with compassion, and being a hearty well-wisher to the sweets of whoring, made no scruple to put herself in the
room

room of her distressed neighbour, who immediately went to keep her word with her gallant. And the dervise, who had heard all this discourse, now no longer accused the shoemaker of cruelty.

In the mean time, however, as luck would have it, the shoemaker waked, and called to his wife; but the surgeon's mate, fearing to be known by her voice, made no answer; this put the shoemaker into such a fury, that he leaped out of the bed, took a knife in his hand, and at one flash cut off, as he thought, his wife's nose, and, holding it in his hand, Here, said he, here is a present for you to send to your wagtail in a corner.

The poor surgeon's wife, though in the utmost agony, durst not so much as sigh for fear; however, quoth she to herself, this is very hard luck, for me to suffer what the shoemaker's wife deserves, while she is toying and dallying in the arms of her lover.

The shoemaker's wife on her return, you may easily imagine, was very much surprized to find her faithful help-mate without a nose; begged her a thousand hearty pardons, unbound her, and tied herself in her place, while the surgeon's mate returned home, carrying her nose in her hand.

Some hours after this, when she thought her husband might hear her, with her hands lifted up to heaven, Most powerful Deity, cried she, who knowest the secrets of all hearts, thou knowest that my husband has abused me without a cause, let him see that I am a woman of reputation, by removing from my face the deformity with which his cruelty has defaced it, and restoring me my nose as it was before. The shoemaker

maker hearing those words, Vile strumpet, cried he, what wicked prayer art thou making? knowest thou not that the prayers of harlots never reach the throne of heaven? Prayers, that would be heard, must issue from a clean heart, and undefiled lips. Villanous and inhuman tyrant, cried his wife, rise and admire the puissance of the Deity, and the excess of his goodness, who, knowing my innocence of the crime for which thou accusest me; is pleased to demonstrate my chastity by restoring me my nose, to the end I may not be looked upon as a woman of dishonour in this world. The shoemaker, believing such a miracle impossible, rises, lights a candle, comes to his wife, and, finding upon her face no mark at all of the cruel fact which he thought he had committed, confessed the injury he had done her to suspect her, begged her pardon, and, by a thousand caresses, strove to make her forget his cruelty.

The surgeon's wife, on the other hand, who was gone home to her lodging, as you may well delieve, in great affliction, crept softly into bed to her husband, who, when he waked, asked her for his case of instruments, that he might go and dress a person he had promised to be with before day. His wife was a long time seeking what her husband demanded, and, when she saw him quite out of patience, gave him a single razor, which put him into such a fury that he flung it at her head, calling her a thousand jades and baggages. It was hardly day when this happened, which favoured the noseless lady's design. Presently therefore she flung herself upon the ground, and filled the air with loud shrieks of murder, murder, which fetched all her neighbours in an instant

stant about her; who, seeing her all bloody, and without a nose, began to cry out shame upon the surgeon, who was so astonished, that he knew not what to say, nor which way to look. He knew not whether it was best for him to deny or confess the fact: however, when morning was come, they hurried the surgeon away before the magistrate, and demanded justice on him for his barbarity. As fortune would have it, however, the dervise also went along with the rabble, and heard the case stated.

After the witnesses were heard, Well, said the judge to the surgeon, what have you to say for yourself? What was the reason that you abused your wife in this horrid manner? To which when the surgeon, seized with astonishment, stood mute, not knowing what to answer, the judge, without farther examination was going to condemn him to death.

On this, the dervise, who had with horror and amazement seen this and the other adventures of his journey, and was as it were possessed with the remembrance of them to such a degree that he could not forbear continually repeating them in his mind, cried out, Hold, O judge! suspend your judgement, and take care what sentence you pronounce; it is neither the thief that stole my garments, nor the rams that killed the fox, nor the harlot that poisoned her lover, nor, lastly, the shoemaker that cut off the surgeon's wife's nose, but every one of the sufferers who have drawn upon themselves all these misfortunes. Then the judge, leaving the surgeon and addressing himself to the dervise, demanded the interpretation of this riddle.

The

The dervife, in anfwer, gave him a full account of all that he had feen; and, moralizing on the whole, Sir, faid he, had I not taken the rich garment out of ambition, the thief had never robbed me; had not the fox thrown himfelf between the rams out of greedinefs, he had not been killed; had not the courtezan gone about to poifon the young gentleman, fhe had not perifhed herfelf; and, had not the furgeon's wife favoured the adultery of the fhoemaker's, fhe had never loft her nofe. And from the whole this fhort leffon is to be learned, that they who commit evil cannot hope for good.

I have made ufe of this fable, faid Kalila to her fpoufe, to fhew you that you have brought thefe troubles upon your own head. It is true, faid Damna, that I am the caufe of them; this I am too fenfible of, but what I defire of you is, to prefcribe me the remedy. I told you from the beginning, replied Kalila, that for my part I would never meddle with your affairs, and now do not intend to trouble myfelf with the cure of your difturbances. Mind your own bufinefs yourfelf, and confider what courfe you have to take, and take it; for, as to me, I have plagues enough of my own, without making myfelf unhappy about the misfortunes that your own follies have brought upon you. Well then, replied Damna, what I fhall do is this, I will ufe all my endeavours to ruin this ox which occafions me all my mifery, and fhall be contented if I but find I have as much wit as the fparrow that revenged himfelf upon the hawk. Kalila upon this defired

him

him to recite that fable, and Damna gave it her in the following words.

---

## FABLE IX.

*The* SPARROW *and the* SPARROW-HAWK.

TWO sparrows had once built their nest under the same hovel, where they had also laid up some small provision for their young ones; but a sparrow-hawk, who had built his nest upon the top of a mountain, at the foot of which this hovel stood, came continually to watch at what time their eggs would be hatched; and, when they were, immediately ate up the young sparrows. This was a most sensible affliction to both the parents. However, they had afterwards another brood, which they hid so among the thatch of the hovel, that the hawk was never able to find them; these therefore they bred up so well, and in so much safety, that they had both of them the pleasure to see them ready to fly. The father and the mother, by their continual chirping, testified for a long time their joy for such a happiness; but, all on a sudden, as the young ones began to be fledged, they fell into a profound melancholy, which was caused through extremity of fear lest the sparrow-hawk should devour these young ones, as he had done the others, as soon as they found their way out of the nest. The eldest of these young sparrows, one day, perceiving this, desired to know of his father the reason of his affliction; which the father having discovered to him, he

made

made answer, that, instead of breaking his heart with sorrow, it much better became him to seek out some way, if possible, to remove so dangerous a neighbour. All the sparrows approved this advice of the young one; and, while the mother flew to get food, the father went another way in search of some cure for his sorrows.' After he had flown about for some time, said he to himself, I know not, alas! what it is I am seeking. Whither shall I fly? and to whom shall I discover my troubles? At length he resolved, not knowing what course to take, to address himself to the first creature he met, and to consult him about his business. This first creature chanced to be a salamander, whose extraordinary shape at first affrighted him: however, the sparrow would not alter his resolution, but accosted and saluted him. The salamander, who was very civil, gave him an obliging reception; and, looking upon him with a fixed eye, Friend, said he, I discover much trouble in thy countenance; if it proceed from weariness, sit down and rest thyself; if from any other cause, let me know it, and, if it be in my power to serve thee, command me. With that the sparrow told his misfortunes in such moving language as raised compassion in the salamander. Well, said he, be of courage, let not these troubles any more perplex thee, I will deliver thee from this wicked neighbour this very night; only shew me his nest, and then go peaceably to roost with thy young ones; this the sparrow accordingly punctually did, and returned the salamander many thanks for being so much concerned for his misfortunes.

No

No sooner was the night come, but the salamander, determining to make good his promise, collected together a number of his fellows, and away they went in a body, with every one a bit of lighted sulphur in their mouths, to the sparrow-hawk's nest, who, not dreaming of any such thing, was surprized by the salamanders, who threw the sulphur into the nest, and burnt the old hawk, with all the young ones.

This fable teaches ye, that whoever has a design to ruin his enemy may possibly bring it about let him be ever so weak. But consider, spouse, cried Kalila, Cohotorbe is the king's chief favourite, and it will be a difficult thing, believe me, to ruin him; where prudent princes have once placed their confidence they seldom withdraw it because of a bare report; and I presume you will not be able to use any other means on this occasion. I will take care however, replied Damna, of this at least, that it shall be represented to the lion, that one of the six great things which cause the ruin of kingdoms, and which indeed is the principal, is to neglect and contemn men of wit and courage. That indeed, replied Kalila, is one very great one; but what, I pray, are the other five. The second, continued Damna, is not to punish the seditious; the third is to be too much given to women, to play, and diversions; the fourth, the accidents attending a pestilence, a famine, or an earthquake; the fifth is being too rash and violent; and the sixth is, the preferring war before peace. You are wise and prudent, spouse, replied Kalila, but let me, though more
simple,

simple, advise thee in this matter: Be not the carver of your own revenge; but consider that whoever meditates mischief commonly brings it at last upon his own head. On the other side, he, that studies his neighbour's welfare, prospers in every thing he undertakes, as you may see by the ensuing fable.

## FABLE X.

### The KING who from a SAVAGE TYRANT became benign and just.

THERE was once, in the eastern part of Egypt, a king, whose reign had long been a course of savage tyranny; long had he ruined the rich, and distressed the poor; so that all his subjects, day and night, implored of heaven to be delivered from him. One day, as he returned from hunting, after he had summoned his people together: Unhappy subjects, says he to them, my conduct has been long unjustifiable in regard to you: but that tyranny, with which I have governed hitherto, is at an end, and I assure you from henceforward you shall live in peace and at ease, and nobody shall dare to oppress you. The people were extremely overjoyed at the good news, and forbore praying against the king.

In a word, this prince made from this time such an alteration in his conduct, that he acquired the title of the Just, and every one began to bless the felicity of his reign. One day, when his subjects were thus settled in happpiness, one

one of his favourites presuming to ask him the reason of so sudden and so remarkable a change, the king gave him this answer: As I rode out hunting the other day, said he, I saw a series of accidents, which threw me into a turn of mind that has produced this happy change; which, believe me, cannot give my people more real satisfaction than it does myself. The things that made this change in me where these; I saw a dog in pursuit of a fox, who, after he had overtaken him, bit off the lower part of his leg; however, the fox, lame as he was, made a shift to escape and get into a hole, and the dog, not able to get him out, left him there: hardly had he gone, however, a hundred paces, when a man threw a great stone at him and cracked his skull; at the same instant the man ran in the way of a horse, that trod upon his foot and lamed him for ever; and, soon after, the horse's foot stuck so fast between two stones, that he broke his ancle-bone in striving to get it out. On seeing these sudden misfortunes befal those who had engaged in doing ill to others, I could not help saying to myself, men are used as they use others: whoever does that which he ought not to do receives what he is not willing to receive.

This example shews you, my dear spouse, that they, who do mischief to others, are generally punished themselves for it when they least expect it: believe me, if you attempt to ruin Cohotorbe, you will repent of it; he is stronger than you, and has more friends. No matter for that, dear spouse, replied Damna, wit is al-

E 2 ways

ways beyond strength, as the following fable will convince you.

## FABLE XI.

### *A* Raven, *a* Fox, *and a* Serpent.

A Raven had once built her nest for many seasons together in a convenient cleft of a mountain; but, however pleasing the place was to her, she had always reason enough to resolve to lay there no more; for, every time she hatched, a serpent came and devoured her young ones. The raven, complaining to a fox that was one of her friends, said to him, Pray tell me, what would you advise me to do to be rid of this serpent? What do you think to do? answered the fox. Why, my present intent is, replied the raven, to go and peck out his eyes when he is asleep, that so he may no longer find the way to my nest. The fox disapproved this design, and told the raven, that it became a prudent person to manage his revenge in such a manner, that no mischief might befal himself in taking it: Never run yourself, says he, into the misfortune that once befel the crane, of which I will tell you the fable.

FABLE

## FABLE XII.

*The* CRANE *and the* CRAY-FISH.

A Crane had once settled her habitation by the side of a broad and deep lake, and lived upon such fish as she could catch in it; these she got in plenty enough for many years; but at length, being become old and feeble, she could fish no longer. In this afflicting circumstance she began to reflect, with sorrow, on the carelessness of her past years; I did ill, said she to herself, in not making in my youth necessary provision to support me in my old age; but, as it is, I must now make the best of a bad market, and use cunning to get a livelihood as I can: with this resolution she placed herself by the water-side, and began to sigh and look mighty melancholy. A cray-fish, perceiving her at a distance, accosted her, and asked her why she appeared so sad? Alas, said she, how can I otherwise choose but grieve, seeing my daily nourishment is like to be taken from me? for I just now heard this talk between two fishermen passing this way: said the one to the other, here is great store of fish, what think you of clearing this pond; to whom his companion answered, no —there is more in such a lake: let us go thither first, and then come hither the day afterwards. This they will certainly perform, and then, added the crane, I must soon prepare for death.

The cray-fish, on this, went to the fish and told them what she had heard: upon which the poor fish, in great perplexity, swam immediately to the crane, and, addressing themselves to her, told her what they had heard, and added, we are now in so great a consternation, that we are come to desire **your** protection. Though you are our enemy, yet the wise tell us, that who make their enemy their sanctuary, m.; assured of being well received: you know full well that we are your daily food; and, if we are destroyed, you, who are too old to travel in search of food, must also perish; we pray you, therefore, for your own sake as well as ours, to consider and tell us what you think is the best course for us to take. To which the crane replied, That which you acquaint me with I heard myself from the mouths of the fishermen; we have no power sufficient to withstand them; nor do I know any other way to secure you but this: it will be many months before they can clear the other pond they are to go about first; and, in the mean time, I can at times, and as my strength will permit me, remove you one after another into a little pond here hard by, where there is very good water, and where the fishermen can never catch you by reason of the extraordinary depth. The fish approved this counsel, and desired the crane to carry them one by one into this pond: nor did she fail to fish up three or four every morning; but she carried them no farther than to the top of a small hill, where she ate them: and thus she feasted herself for a while.

But, one day, the cray-fish, having a desire to see this delicate pond, made known her curiosity to the crane, who, bethinking herself that the cray-fish was her most mortal enemy, resolved to get rid of her at once, and murder her as she

had

had done the reſt. With this deſign ſhe flung the cray-fiſh upon her neck, and flew towards the hill. But when they came near the place, the cray-fiſh, ſpying at a diſtance the ſmall bones of her ſlaughtered companions, miſtruſted the crane's intentions; and, laying hold of a fair opportunity, got her neck in her claw, and graſped it ſo hard, that ſhe fairly ſaved herſelf, and ſtrangled the crane.

This example, ſays the fox, ſhews you, that crafty, tricking, people often become victims to their own cunning. The raven, returning thanks to the fox for his good advice, ſaid, I ſhall not, by any means, neglect your wholeſome inſtructions; but what ſhall I do? Why, replied the fox, you muſt ſnatch up ſomething that belongs to ſome ſtout man or other, and let him ſee what you do, to the end he may follow you: which, that he may eaſily do, do you fly ſlowly; and, when you are juſt over the ſerpent's hole, let fall the thing that you hold in your beak or talons, whatever it be; for then, the perſon that follows you, ſeeing the ſerpent come forth, will not fail to knock him on the head. The raven did as the fox deſired him, and by that means was delivered from the ſerpent.

What cannot be done by ſtrength, ſaid Damna, is to be performed by policy. It is very true, replied Kalila; but the miſchief here is, that the ox has more policy than you. He will, by his prudence, fruſtrate all your projects, and, before you can pluck one hair from his tail, will flea off your ſkin. I know not whether you have ever heard of the fable of the rabbit, the fox, and the wolf; if not, I will tell it you, that you may make your advantage of it in the present case.

## FABLE XIII.

*The* RABBIT, *the* FOX, *and the* WOLF.

A Hungry wolf once spied a rabbit feeding at the foot of a tree, and was soon preparing to seize him. The rabbit, perceiving him, would have saved his life by flight; but the wolf threw himself in his way, and stopped his escape: so that, seeing himself in the power of the wolf, submissive and prostrate at his feet, he gave him all the good words he could think of. I know, said he, that the king of all creatures wants a supply to appease his hunger, and that he is now ranging the fields in search of food; but I am but an insignificant morsel for his royal stomach: therefore let him be pleased to take my information. About a furlong from hence lives a fox that is fat and plump, and whose flesh is as white as a capon's: such a prey will do your majesty's business. If you please I will go and give him a visit, and engage him to come forth out of his hole: then, if he prove to your liking, you may devour him; if not it will be my glory that I had the honour of not dying in vain, but being a small breakfast for your majesty.

Thus, over-persuaded, the wolf gave the rabbit leave to seek out the fox, and followed him at the heels. The rabbit left the wolf at the entrance of the hole, and crept in himself, overjoyed

joyed that he had such an opportunity to revenge himself on the fox, from whom he had received an affront, which he had for a long time pretended to have forgot. He made him a low congee, and gave him great protestations of his friendship. On the other side, the fox was no less obliging in his answers to the rabbit's civilities, and asked him what good wind had blown him thither. Only the great desire I had to see your worship, replied the rabbit, and there is one of my relations at the door, who is no less ambitious to kiss your hands, but he dares not enter without your permission. The fox, on this, mistrusting there was something more than ordinary in all this civility, said to himself, I shall find the bottom of all this presently, and then, if it prove as I suspect, I will take care to pay this pretended friend of mine in his own coin. However, not seeming to take any notice of what he suspected, Sir, said he to the rabbit, your friend shall be most welcome, he does me too much honour——but, added he, I must entreat you to let me put my chamber in a little better order to receive him. The rabbit too much persuaded of the good success of his enterprize, Puh, puh, said he, my relation is one that never stands upon ceremonies, and so went out to give the wolf notice that the fox was fallen into the snare. The wolf thought he had the fox fast already, and the rabbit believed himself quite out of danger, as having done the wolf such a piece of good service. But the fox was too sharp sighted to be thus trepanned out of his life. He had, at the entrance of his hole, a very deep trench, which he had digged on purpose to guard him against surprizes of this nature. Presently,

sently, therefore, he took away the planks, which he had laid for the convenience of those that came to visit him, covered the trench with a little earth and straw, and set open a back door in case of necessity; and, having thus prepared all things, he desired the rabbit and his friend to walk in. But, instead of the success of their plot, the two visitors found themselves, before they expected it, in the bottom of a very deep pit, and the wolf, imagining that the rabbit had a hand in the contrivance, in the heat of his fury tore him to pieces.

By this you see, that finesse and policy signify nothing, where you have persons of wit and prudence to deal with. It is very true, said Damna, but the ox is now proud of his preferment, and thoughtless of danger, at least from me; for he has not the least suspicion of my hatred. A rabbit, wiser than that you have been speaking of, once undertook the ruin of a lion, and you shall see how he brought it about.

## FABLE XIV.
### The LION and the RABBIT.

IN the neighbourhood of Mianstol* there was a very delightful meadow, where several wild beasts had taken up their habitations, by reason of the pleasantness of the place. Among those creatures there was a furious lion, who disturbed the peace of all the rest with his continual

---

* Mianstol is a large tract of country on the banks of the Ganges, uninhabited, except by a great number of wild beasts.

murders.

murders. In order to remedy this dreadful evil, one day they met all together, went to wait upon the lion, and layed their cafe before him; that they were his fubjects, and, in confequence, that it no way became him to make, every day, fuch dreadful flaughters among them, of whole families together. You feek after us, added they, to rule over us; but, though we are proud of a king of fo much valour, yet, in fear, we avoid you; would you live peaceably with us, and enjoy your quiet by letting us alone, we would bring you every morning fufficient and delicate food, nor fhould you ever want to crown' your meals with a flafket of tame and wild fowl, and you fhould, yourfelf, never be put to the toil of hunting. The lion readily accepted this propofal, and the beafts caft lots every morning, and he, upon whom the lot fell, was appointed to hunt for the lion.

One day the lot fell upon a rabbit, who feeing he could not avoid it, after he had fummoned all the beafts together, faid to them, You fee how miferable a life it is we lead here; either we muft be eaten ourfelves, or fpend our labour to feed a churlifh mafter. Now hear what I have to propofe; do you but ftand by me, and I will certainly deliver you from this cruel tyrant that reigns over us. To this they all unanimoufly anfwered, that they would do their utmoft. Upon this the rabbit ftayed in his hole till the hour of dinner was paft, and made no provifion for the lion. By this time the lion's anger augmented with his appetite; he lafhed the ground with his tail, and at length perceiving the rabbit, Whence come you, faid he, and what are my fubjects doing? Do they

they suppose, I accepted their proposal, and spared their lives, to be kept without victuals by their idleness? Be assured, if I wait much longer, they shall, some of them, severely pay for it. May it please pour majesty hear me, answered the rabbit, bowing to him with a profound respect; your subjects, sacred sir, have not been wanting in their duty; they sent me hither to bring your majesty your accustomed provision; but I met a lion by the way who took it from me. I told him, when he seized it, that it was for the king: to which he most insolently answered, that there was no other king in this country but himself. Struck dumb with this monstrous behaviour, I left him, and ran to inform your majesty of this heinous piece of insolence. The lion, on this, furiously turning about his burning eyes, cried out, Who is this audacious usurper that dares to lay his paw upon my food, which my subjects had laboured to provide for me? can'st thou shew me where the audacious traitor lives? Yes sir, replied the rabbit, if you will be pleased to follow me. The lion, breathing revenge and destruction, followed the wily rabbit; and when they came to a well that was full of clear water, sir, said the rabbit, your enemy lives in this well, I dare not shew him you, but only be pleased to look in yourself, and you will see him: have a care, however, that you are not first assailed. With that the lion went stalking to the well, and, seeing the reflection of his own image, which he took to be another lion in the water that had devoured his food, enflamed with anger he flung himself into the well to encounter this mortal foe, and there was drowned himself.

This

This fable shews you, that a strong person may he destroyed by one that is much weaker, when he is not mistrusted. Well, well, said Kalila, if you can ruin the ox without doing the lion any harm, go on and prosper; if not, I advise you to give over your enterprise: for it does not become a subject, for his own private interest and repose, to suffer any mischief to befal his prince.

Here the confabulation between Damna and Kalila ended; and Damna, having taken leave of his wife, absented himself for some time from the lion's court. Afterwards he returned, and affecting an air of sadness before his majesty, Honest Damna, said the king to him, whence comest thou? where hast thou been this long time? Any news abroad? Yes, sir, answered Damna with a deep sigh, news indeed; such news as I dread to speak, yet such as your majesty ought to hear. On this the king, starting for fear, cried out, What is it? I beg your majesty, replied Damna, since you will hear it, will be pleased to grant me a private audience. Affairs of importance ought never to be delayed, replied the king; and so, commanding the room to be immediately cleared, ordered Damna to speak what he had to say. It is requisite, said that wily minister, that the bearer of ill news should have the address to give it an allay; and it is also most necessary, that he, to whom it is reported, should be able to judge whether the person who makes the report be worthy to be credited, or whether he speak falsely and for the sake of his own interest; and, if he be

worthy

worthy to be believed, he ought to be entirely confided in, when his difcourfe may be advantageous to the public, or, what is yet of greater confequence, to the fovereign himfelf. On this the lion interrupting him, Thou knoweft, faid he, that I have experienced thy fidelity, and therefore fpeak boldly what thou haft to fay. The purity of my intentions, continued Damna, have made me to affume this boldnefs, and I am more than happy to be known to your majefty. I queftion not thy zeal, faid the lion; but pr'ythee come to the news which it fo much concerns me to know.

When Damna perceived the good fuccefs of his flatteries, and that the king had confidence in him, he thus began his difcourfe. Sir, faid he, I am forry to relate it, but my excellently efteemed friend, and your majefty's great favourite, Cohotorbe, has daily conferences with the grandees and chieftains of your army, and I know that in them he improves every circumftance, as much as lies in his power, to your majefty's prejudice; which makes me believe he has fome defign upon your facred perfon. I grieve to tell this, and am not lefs aftonifhed than angry, when I reflect that he fhould fo ungratefully abufe your favours, and the particular friendfhip with which you are pleafed to honour him. Damna, cried the lion, take care what thou fayeft; thou art accufing one of whom I have a fettled good opinion: but, if this be true, what courfe is to be taken? Sir, replied Damna, there are two forts of people in the world, the one fage and prudent, the other rafh and inconfiderate. The laft are always at a lofs, when any accident be-

fals

fals them; the other always foresee things, and therefore nothing moves them, whatever happens. We ought, sir, to imitate their prudence, and secure ourselves from danger, so soon as we have the least notice or intimation of it. There is also, besides these, yet another sort of people, who, I have observed, never truly foresee danger; but, however, know how to take the proper courses when it presents itself: and these three characters put me in mind of the fable of the three fish, which I would tell your majesty, did I not fear it would offend your patience. The lion, on this, commanded Damna to let him hear it out; so Damna thus proceeded.

## FABLE XV.

### *The two* FISHERMEN *and the three* FISH.

THERE was once, in your majesty's dominions, a certain pond, the water of which was very clear, and emptied itself into a neighbouring river. This pond was in a quiet place; it was remote from the highway, and there were in it three fish; the one of which was prudent, the second had but little wit, and the third was a mere fool. One day, by chance, two fishermen, in their walks, perceiving this pond, made up to it, and no sooner observed these three fish, which were large and fat, but they went and fetched their nets to take them. The fish suspecting, by what they saw of the fishermen, that they intended no less than their destruction,

be-

began to be in a world of terror. The prudent fish immediately resolved what course to take: he threw himself out of the pond, through the little channel that opened into the river, and so made his escape. The next morning the two fishermen returned; they made it their first business to stop up all the passages, to prevent the fish from getting out, and were making preparations for taking them. The half-witted fish now heartily repented that he had not followed his companion; at length, however, he bethought himself of a stratagem; he appeared upon the surface of the water with his belly upward, and feigned to be dead. The fisherman also, having taken him up, thought him really what he counterfeited himself to be, so threw him again into the water. And the last, which was the foolish fish, seeing himself pressed by the fishermen, sunk down to the bottom of the pond, shifted up and down from place to place, but could not avoid, at last, falling into their hands, and was that day made part of a public entertainment.

This example, continued Damna, shews your majesty, that you ought to prevent Cohotorbe from doing the mischief he intends, by making yourself master of his life, before he have yours at his command. What you say is very agreeable to reason, said the king, but I cannot yet believe that Cohotorbe, upon whom I have heaped so many favours, should be so perfidious as you represent him. Why, it is most true, replied Damna, that he never received any thing but kindness from your majesty; but, *what is bred in the bone will never*

*never out of the flesh; neither can any thing come out of a vessel but what is put into it.* Of which the following fable is a sufficient proof.

---

## FABLE XVI.

### The SCORPION and the TORTOISE.

A Tortoise and scorpion had once contracted a great intimacy, and bound themselves in such a tie of friendship, that the one could not live without the other. These inseparable companions, one day, finding themselves obliged to change their habitation, travelled together; but, in their way, meeting with a large and deep river, the scorpion making a stop, said to the tortoise, My dear friend, you are well provided for what we see before us, but how shall I get over this water? Never trouble yourself, my dear friend, for that, replied the tortoise, I will carry you upon my back secure from all danger. The scorpion on this, without hesitation, got upon the back of the tortoise, who immediately took water and began to swim. But he was hardly got half way across the river, when he heard a terrible rumbling upon his back, which made him ask the scorpion what he was doing? Doing! replied the scorpion, why I am whetting my sting, to try whether I can bore this horny cuirass of yours, that covers your flesh like a shield from all injuries. O ungrateful wretch, cried the tortoise, wouldst thou, at a time when I am giving thee such a demonstration of my

friendship,

friendship, wouldst thou, at such a time, pierce with thy venomous sting the defence that nature has given me, and take away my life?

It is well, however, I have it in my power both to save myself and reward thee as thou deservest; so saying, he sunk his back to some depth under water, threw off the scorpion, and left him to pay his life, the just forfeit of his monstrous ingratitude. Had he not destroyed his ungrateful favourite, in this manner, royal sir, continued Damna, his own life had paid for it; and it is a good and most just general rule, that the wicked are never to be favoured. You urge me too hard upon this subject, said the lion, and I cannot but think that, were Cohotorbe capable of so much perfidiousness, he would certainly have shewn his malicious intentions before. Never trust to that, replied Damna, he carries on his design with more prudence. He will not, royal sir, attack your majesty's person openly and publicly himself; no, but he will cajole your whole court, and delude them into his interests, and then take his own time to destroy your sacred person, and, openly avowing his guilt, perhaps, set himself up for king in your place. Just heaven keep me from seeing such a day! providence defend me from such masters! You say something indeed now, said the lion, interrupting him; but, now I know him guilty, how shall we find a fair pretence to be rid of him? Let me alone for that, replied Damna, a faithless subject must be punished.

These amusements of the subtle fox made such an impression on the mind of the king, that he at length told Damna he was come to a resolution to admit Cohotorbe no more into his presence,

fence, but to banish him altogether from his court, after he had upbraided him with his ingratitude, and let him know the reason of his fall. This resolution, however, was far enough from being pleasing to Damna; a guilty conscience never can have rest: he feared that, if the king once came to talk with Cohotorbe, all his villany would be discovered. On this, said he to the lion, Sir, if I may continue my boldness of speaking to your majesty, I have heard, from persons of understanding, that a prince ought never to inflict public punishment upon faults committed in secret; nor secretly to chastise public crimes: therefore, seeing Cohotorbe is a secret transgressor, he must be privately punished. No, replied the lion, it is a great piece of injustice to punish any one before he be told the reason of his punishment. To satisfy yourself of his guilt, replied Damna, it will be sufficient, that once for all you make him sensible of your displeasure, and give him a cold reception: his conscience will upbraid him with his perfidiousness at the same instant, and he will no longer doubt but that you are preparing for him his due reward; and you will perceive him accordingly disturbed and agitated in his mind, which will be an evident proof of the truth of my suspicions. If it prove so, replied the lion, I shall soon be convinced of his treason.

Damna, now seeing the king prepared to his heart's desire, went to Cohotorbe, and made him a low bow. To whom, the ox, after many caresses, said, My good old friend, what is the reason that you come to see me no oftener? Is it because you think me no longer one of your friends?

friends? Though I have been absent for some time, replied Damna, yet, believe me, I have still preserved you in my thoughts. But why, replied the ox, did you retire from the court? For this plain reason, replied Damna, because I love my liberty; and, when we are in the king's presence, we tremble for fear, as always being under restraint. If I mistake not, friend, replied Cohotorbe, you look as if you were not satisfied with the king, and were afraid of some misfortune or foul play. Indeed you have guessed but too well the cause of my uneasiness, answered Damna; I tremble, and am as troubled as you can conceive me to be; but it is for your sake, friend, and not for my own, that I am in this perplexity. Poor Cohotorbe, terribly frighted at this answer, quaking for fear, says to Damna, My dear friend, let me know the danger that threatens me, that, if possible, I may guard against it. To this Damna, with a look of great compassion, replied, It is but just, friend, that you should know your danger, nor should I act consistently with that friendship I have ever professed to you not to acquaint you with it: the truth therefore is this: a friend of mine has intrusted me with a private discourse which passed some days ago, between the king and a great person who has no kindness for your lordship. Said the king to this great person, *I have been considering that Cohotorbe is now very fat and of no use to us; and, as I must a few days hence, feast all the lords of my court, I think the cheapest way will be to roast this ox alive and whole for their entertainment.* I tremble to repeat this; but, as I knew it, I could not but inform you of it, and

bring

bring you the news to convince you that I am your real friend, and to affist you, as far as lies in my power, to avoid the danger. Cohotorbe was aftonifhed at this piece of difmal intelligence: But by what device, faid he, fhall I be able to efcape this intended cruelty of the king? alas, good heaven is my witnefs, I never gave him the leaft occafion to ufe me fo feverely: certainly I muft have fome private enemy who has falfely accufed me behind my back, and incenfed him without a caufe againſt me: and a prince, who difcards and punifhes a fervant on fuch grounds, is like the drake, who feeing the refemblance of the moon in the water, thought it to be fome extraordinary fifh, and, deluded with that error, dived feveral times to catch it; but, mad to fee that all his efforts proved vain, in a violent rage came out of the water, fwearing never to return to that element again: and after that, though he were never fo hungry, would never dive more after any fifh, believing it to be only the light of the moon: but for me, unhappy that I am, backbiters and flatterers have fo prepoſſeſſed the lion againſt me, that, whatever I do henceforward to pleafe him, he will ftill believe that I only diffemble. I know not what to fay, or how to advife in this cafe, replied Damna, the king may fee his error, and alter his mind; but then, on the other fide, being abfolute in his power, he may, without being bound to give any reafon for it, condemn you to death. It is moſt true, replied Cohotorbe, that princes often feek the deftruction of thofe who feem their greateſt favourites. And many, who envy the grandeur and eafe of a court-life, know not the dangerous

accidents

accidents that attend it. As you may learn by the enfuing fable.

## FABLE XVII.

### The FALCON and the HEN.

OF all the animals I was ever acquainted with, said a falcon once to a hen, you are the moſt unmindful of benefits, and the moſt ungrateful. Why, what ingratitude replied the hen, have you ever obſerved in me? Can there be a greater peace of ingratitude, replied the falcon, than that which you commit in regard to men? By day they ſeek out every nouriſhment to fat you; and, in the night, you have a place always ready to rooſt in, where they take care that your chamber be cloſe barred up, that nothing may trouble your repoſe: nevertheleſs, when they would catch you, you forget all their goodneſs to you, and baſely endeavour to eſcape their hands; which is what I never do, I that am a wild creature, no way obliged to them, and a bird of prey: upon the meaneſt of their careſſes I grow tame, ſuffer myſelf to be taken, and never eat but upon their fiſts. All this is very true, replied the hen; but I find you know not the reaſon of my flight; you never ſaw a falcon upon the ſpit; but I have ſeen a thouſand hens dreſt with all manner of ſauces.

I have recited this fable to ſhew you, that often they, who are ambitious of a court-life, know not
the

the inconveniences of it. I believe, friend, said Damna, that the lion seeks your life for no other reason but because he is jealous of your virtues. The fruit-trees only, replied Cohotorbe, are subject to have their branches broken; nightingales are caged because they sing more pleasantly than other birds; and we pluck the peacock's feathers from their tails for no other reason but because they are beautiful. Merit alone is, therefore, too often the source and origin of our misfortunes. However, I am not afraid of whatever contrivances the malice of wicked people can make to my prejudice; but shall endeavour to submit to what I cannot prevent, and imitate the nightingale in the following fable.

## FABLE XVIII.

*The* NIGHTINGALE *and the* COUNTRYMAN.

A Certain countryman had a rose-bush in his garden, which he made his sole pleasure and delight. Every morning he went to look upon it, in the season of its flowering, and see his roses ready to blow. One day, as he was admiring, according to his custom, the beauty of the flowers, he spied a nightingale, perched upon one of the branches near a very fine flower, and plucking off the leaves of it one after another. This put him into so great a passion, that the next day he laid a snare for the nightingale in revenge for the wrong; in which he succeeded so well, that he took the bird and immediately put her in a cage. The nightingale, very melancholy

choly to see herself in that condition, with a mournful voice asked the countryman the reason of her slavery. To whom he replied, Knowest thou not that my whole delight was in those flowers, which thou wast wantonly destroying? Every leaf which thou pluckedst from that rose was as a drop of blood from my heart. Alas! replied the nightingale, you use me very severely for having cropt a few leaves from a rose; but expect to be used harshly in the other world, for afflicting me in this manner; for there all people are used after the same manner as they here use the other animals. The countryman, moved with these words, gave the nightingale her liberty again; for which she, willing to thank him, said, Since you have had compassion in your nature, and have done me this favour, I will repay your kindness in the manner it deserves. Know therefore, continued she, that, at the foot of yonder tree, there lies buried a pot full of gold, go and take it, and heaven bless you with it. The countryman digged about the tree, and, finding the pot, astonished at the nightingale's sagacity in discovering it; I wonder, said he to her, that, being able to see this pot, which was buried under ground, you could not discover the net that was spread for your captivity? Know you not, replied the nightingale, that, however sharp-sighted or prudent we are, we can never escape our destiny.

By this example you see that, when we are conscious of our own innocence, we are wholly to resign ourselves up to our fate. It is very true, replied Damna; the lion, however, according

to

to the most just observation of the captive nightingale in your fable, in seeking your destruction, cannot but incur divine punishment; and, desirous as he is to augment his grandeur by your fall, I am apt to to think that what once befel the hunter will be his destiny.

## FABLE XIX.

*The* HUNTER, *the* FOX, *and the* LEOPARD.

A Certain hunter once, said Damna, pursuing his discourse, espied, in the middle of a field, a fox, who looked with so engaging an aspect, and had on a skin so fair and lovely, that he had a great desire to take him alive. With this intent he found out his hole, and just before the entrance into it dug a very deep trench, which he covered with slender twigs and straw, and, having laid on it a piece of smoking lamb's flesh, just cut up, went and hid himself in a corner, out of sight. The fox returning to his hole, and observing, at a distance, what the hunter had left for his breakfast, presently ran to see what dainty morsel it was. When he came to the trench, he would fain have been tasting the delicate entertainment; but the fear of some treachery would not permit him to fall to: and, in short, finding he had strong reasons to suspect some ill design towards him, he was cunning enough to remove his lodging, and take up other quarters. In a moment after he was gone, as fortune would have it, came a hungry leopard, who, being tempted by the

the favory odour of the yet warm and fmoking flefh, made fuch hafte to fall to, that he tumbled into the trench. The hunter, hearing the noife of the falling leopard, immediately threw himfelf into the trench, without looking into it, never queftioning but that it was the fox he had taken; but there found, inftead of him, the leopard, who tore him in pieces, and devoured him.

This fable teaches us, that, however earneftly we may wifh for any event, prudence and wifdom ought to regulate our defires. I did very ill indeed, replied Cohotorbe, to accept the lion's offer of favour and friendfhip, and now heartily wifh I had been content with an humbler fortune. It is not enough, replied Damna, interrupting him, to repent and bewail your paft life; your bufinefs is now to endeavour to moderate the lion's paffion. I am affured of his natural good-will to me, replied Cohotorbe; but traitors and flatterers will do their utmoft to change his favour into hatred, and I am afraid they will bring about their defigns. Do not you remember that the wolf, the fox, and the raven, once ruined the camel.

## FABLE XX.

### *The* WOLF, *the* FOX, *the* RAVEN, *and the* CAMEL.

IN former ages, continued Cohotorbe, there were a crafty raven, a fubtle fox, and a bloody wolf, who put themfelves into the fervice

vice of a lion, that held his court in a wood, near a certain not-much-frequented highway. Near this place, a merchant's camel once, quite tired with long travel, got rid of his burden, and lay down to rest himself, and, if possible, preserve his life. In a few days after, having recovered his strength, he rose up, and, ignorant of the governor of these territories, entered into the lion's wood, with a design to feed. But, before he had spent an hour in travelling into it, he was astonished at the appearance of the lion, whose majestic gate and aspect soon informed our traveller that he was monarch of the place. The camel, who, at first sight, expected nothing but to be devoured, was rejoiced to find this, and humbly offered him his service. The lion accepted it; and, after he knew by what accident he came into the place, asked him what he would choose to do? Whatever your majesty pleases, replied the camel, very submissively. Thou art at thy liberty, replied the lion, to return, if thou likest it, and be the slave of thy former master; or, if thou wilt rather live with me, thou hast my sacred and inviolable promise that thou shalt be secure from all injuries. The camel was very glad of this, and remained with the lion, doing nothing but feed without disturbance, so that he soon became plump and fat.

One day, after this, the lion, in his hunting, met an elephant, with whom he encountered; and, returning wounded to the wood, at length he was starved to death. While he lay on his death-bed, however, the raven, the wolf, and the fox, who lived only upon what the lion left after he had been at the field, fell into a deep melancholy; which the lion perceiving, he said to them, I am more sorry for your sadness than for my own wounds. Go, and see if you can meet with any venison in the purlieus adjoining; if you do, return and give me notice, and, notwithstanding my wounds, I will go and seize it for you. Upon this, away they went, left the lion, and held a council all three together. Said the wolf, if I may speak among you, friends, what good does this camel do here? we have no correspondence with him; nor does the lion get any thing by him; let us kill him, and he will keep us alive two or three days, and, by that time, the king may, perhaps, be cured of his wounds. This advice, however, though hunger much pleaded in its favour, did not much please the fox, who affirmed that the camel's life could not be justly taken away, since the lion had given his word and solemn promise that he should live unmolested in the wood; for that such an action would render the king odious to all posterity, who would look upon him as a perfidious monarch, who gave protection to a stranger in his dominions only to put him to death without a cause, whenever he could make an advantage of his destruction.

On this, the raven, who had as hungry a belly as the wolf, together with a great deal of wit and as much malice, took upon him to reconcile both these opinions, saying, that there might be a fair pretence found to colour the death of the camel. Stay here, continued he, till I return, and I will bring you the lion's consent for his destruction. So saying, away he went to the lion; and, when he came in his presence, making a profound reverence, and putting on a starved and
meager

meager look, said, May it please your majesty to hear me a few words: we are almost famished to death, and so weak that we can hardly crawl along; but we have found out a remedy for all this, and, if your majesty will but give leave, have contrived how we shall have a feast. What is your remedy? answered the lion, hardly able to open his jaws for weakness and anguish; and what the feast you propose yourselves? To whom the raven replied, Sir, the camel, whom you once met in the wood, lives like a hermit in your kingdom; he never comes near us, nor is he good for any thing but to satisfy our hunger. And, in regard your majesty wants good and wholesome diet in your present weak condition, I am surgeon enough to venture to assure you, that camel's flesh must be very proper for you. The lion, who was of a truly noble disposition, was highly incensed at this proposal of the raven, and very passionately exclaimed, Oh! what a wicked and treacherous age is this! vile and cunning as you are, for I have long known you, Corvo, (for so was the raven called,) how can all your sophistry prove it lawful in a king to be faithless, and violate ascertained promises? Sir, replied the raven, far be it from me to attempt to prove that; but, may it please your majesty, I cannot but remember, upon this most urgent occasion, that great casuists hold it for a maxim, that a single person may be sacrificed to the welfare of a whole nation. Or, should not this be entirely satisfactory to your majesty, perhaps there may be some expedient found to disengage you from your promise. Upon that, the lion bowed down his head with fatigue and anguish, as if to con-

*sider*

sider of it, and the raven returned to his companions, to whom he related what discourse had passed between the king and him. And now, said he, let us go to the camel, and inform him of the unfortunate accident that has befallen the king, and of his being likely to starve; and then lay before him, that, since we have spent the greatest part of our lives in peace and plenty under the king's reign, it is but just that some of us now should surrender up our own to prolong his days.

In pursuance of this discourse, we will engage the camel to accompany us, and go to the king and offer him our three carcases; striving, at the same time, which shall be most free of his flesh to serve his majesty for his present nourishment. The camel, perhaps, will then be willing to follow our example, and offer to sacrifice himself in the same manner, and then we'll take him at his word. This they all readily agreed to; and, in short, acted their parts so well, that they took the camel with them to the king, to whom the raven thus addressed himself: Sir, said he, seeing your health is of much more consequence to the public good, and more precious to us than our own lives, suffer me to shew the just sense I have of my duty, by offering up my own body to you, to appease your raging hunger. What a goodly collation you offer to his majesty! cried the fox, well instructed in the part he was to act in this design; you, that have only a little skin and three or four dry bones, are a precious bit to satisfy the king, who, I warrant you, could feed at this time like a glutton after a three days fast. I have better flesh, and more sub-
stantial

stantial than yours, and have so much true sense of my duty (as I hope every one of his majesty's subjects has, especially those who, like us, have tasted of his favours) that I am as desirous as yourself to approve my gratitude and love to my sovereign. And, turning to the lion, sir, said he, let me entreat your majesty to eat me. After these, the wolf played his part. Sir, said he, your majesty must have more solid diet to refresh your hungry stomach than these can afford you, and I think myself a banquet much more proper to regale you. The camel, on this, unwilling to appear less affectionate than the rest, when it came to his turn, All you three, said he, are not enough to satisfy the king's hunger; but, though he had not eaten a mouthful these three days, I alone am sufficient to restore him to his health. Then said all the rest, this camel speaks reason, his flesh is excellent, dainty, and worth your majesty's taste. How happy will he be to leave to posterity such an example of zeal and generosity! And, so saying, they all fell upon him, and tore him to pieces before he could speak another word.

This fable shews you, that, when several conspirators combine together in the contrivance of an enterprize, they easily bring it to pass. You are perfectly in the right, said Damna; and, for my part, were I in your condition, I would defend my life; and, if I must perish, fall like a warrior, not like a victim of justice at the gallows. He, that dies with his sword in his hand, renders himself famous. It is not good to begin a war; but, when we are attacked, it is

F 4    ignominious

ignominious to surrender ourselves cowardly into the enemy's hand. This is right and proper counsel, replied Cohotorbe; but we ought to know our strength before we engage in a combat: for, if we attack our enemy rashly and imprudently, we may, too late, perhaps, remember the famous story of the angel-ruler of the sea, which I will tell you.

## FABLE XXI.

### *The* ANGEL-RULER *of the* SEA, *and two Birds called* GERANDI*.

TWO birds, of that kind called gerandi, continued Cohotorbe, once lived together upon the shores of the Indian sea. After they had long enjoyed the pleasures of conjugal affection, when it was near the season for laying eggs, said the female to the male, it is time for me to choose a proper place wherein to produce my young ones. To whom the male replied, this, where we now are, is, I think, a very good place. No, replied the female, this cannot do; for, the sea may hereafter swell beyond these bounds, and the waves carry away my eggs. That can never be, said the male, nor dares the angel-ruler of the sea do me an injury; for, if he should, he knows I would certainly call him to account. You

---

* Gerandi are birds of the East Indes, which lay their eggs in the sands on the sea-shore, and sit four weeks.

must

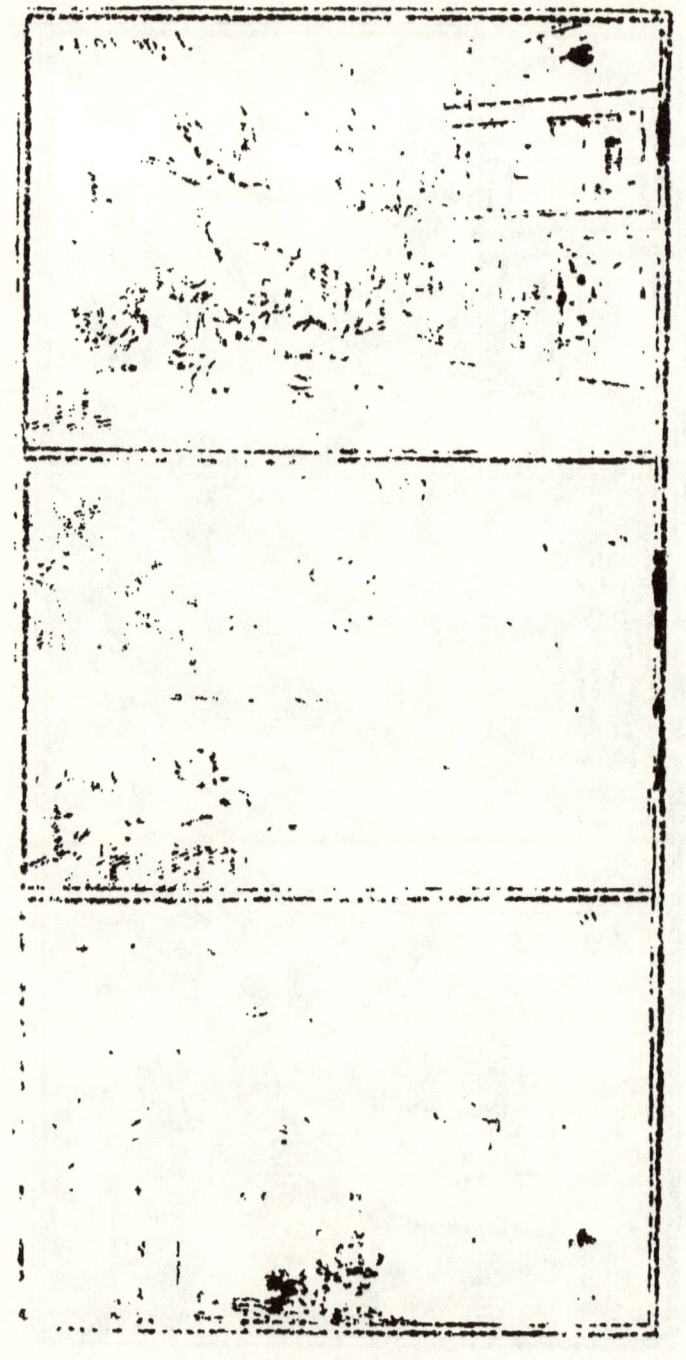

must never boast, replied the female, of a thing which you are not able to perform. What comparison is there between you and the prince of the sea? Take my advice: avoid such quarrels; and, if you despise my admonitions, beware you are not ruined by your obstinacy. Remember the misfortune that befel the tortoise. It is a story I have not heard, replied the male; pray tell it me.

## FABLE XXII.

### *The* TORTOISE *and two* DUCKS.

THERE was a tortoise, continued the female, that lived in a pond with some ducks, her old companions, in full content and great felicity, for many years. But, at length, there happened so dry a season, that there was at last no water in the pond. The ducks, upon this, finding themselves constrained to remove to some other habitation, went to the tortoise to take their leaves of him. The tortoise, in terror for his impending destruction, upbraided them for leaving him in the time of his calamity, and besought them to carry him along with them. To whom the ducks replied, Be assured it is a great trouble to us that we must leave you in this condition, but we are constrained to it for our own preservation: and, as to what you propose to us, to take you with us, we have a long journey to make, and you can never follow us, because you cannot fly. On this condition, however, it is possible for us to save you,

if

if you can only be enough your own friend to follow our advice, and keep a strict and perfect silence; and, on this condition, if you will promise us not to speak a word by the way, we will carry you. But we shall meet with some that will talk to us, and then it is ten to one but you will be twatling; and, if you are, remember that we now tell you, beforehand, it will be your destruction. No, answered the tortoise, fear me not; I will do whatever you would have me. Things being thus settled, the ducks ordered the tortoise to take a little stick and hold it by the middle fast in his mouth; and then, exhorting him to keep steady, they took the stick by each end, and so raised him up. Thus they carried him along in triumph; but it was not long before, as they flew over a village, the inhabitants, wondering at the novelty of the sight, fell to shouting with all their might; this made such a noise that the tortoise grew impatient to be twatling; and, at length, not able to keep silence any longer, he was going to wish the people's mouths sewed up, for making such a clamour; but, so soon as he opened his mouth to vent his curses, he let go the stick, and so fell to the ground and killed himself.

This example shews us, spouse, said the female gerandi, that we ought not to despise the exhortation of friends. I have heard your fable, said the male, and all that I shall say in answer to it is this, *They who want courage are no way capable of great performances.* Be governed by me; I have as earnest a desire of preserving our young ones as yourself, yet I am bold to say let

us

us hatch our young ones in this place; and be assured, that the angel-ruler of the sea dares do us no harm. The female, on this, obeyed, and built her nest accordingly in the sand by the sea-side. But, within a day or two after, the ocean swelling, the waves overturned the nest, and the ruler of the sea took the eggs. The female, on this misfortune, addressing herself to the male, said, I told you that you were too vain-glorious to dare to out-brave a power which it became you rather to revere; but, now he has done this injury, let us see how you will revenge yourself? Depend upon it, replied the male, I will make him restore your eggs: and so saying, without delay, he flew to all the birds, one after another, told them the story, and craved their aid to revenge himself upon the ruler of the sea. All the birds promised their succour to the gerandi, and went with him to the griffin, and threatened to acknowledge him no longer for their king if he did not head them in this enterprize. The griffin, as tenacious of the right of his subjects as revengeful in his own nature, readily engaged in the war, and immediately flew before them, and they beset the ruler of the sea's palace; who, seeing such an infinite number of birds, in great terror and affright, came out to them, and restored the eggs.

An enemy, said Damna, I very well know, is at no time to be despised. However, replied Cohotorbe, I will not begin the combat; but, if the lion attack me, I will endeavour to defend myself. Well, answered Damna, that you may know when to be upon your guard, let me give you this caution: when you see him lash the ground

ground with his tail, and roll his eyes angrily about, you may be fure he will immediately be upon you. I thank you for your advice, replied Cohotorbe, and, when I obferve the figns which you have, fo like a friend, informed me of, I fhall prepare myfelf to receive him.

Here they parted; and Damna, overjoyed at the fuccefs of his enterprize, ran to Kalila, who afked him how his defign went forward. I thank my fates, cried Damna, I am juft going to triumph over my enemy. After this fhort confabulation, the two foxes went to court, where, foon after, Cohotorbe arrived.

The lion no fooner beheld him, but he thought him guilty: and Cohotorbe, cafting his eyes upon the lion, made no queftion, from what he faw, but that his majefty had refolved his ruin: fo that both the one and the other manifefting thofe figns which Damna had defcribed to each, there began a moft terrible combat, wherein the lion killed the ox, but not, however, without a great deal of trouble and hazard. When all was over, O! what a wicked creature thou art! cried Kalila to Damna, thou haft here, for thine own fake, endangered the king's life: thy end will be miferable for contriving fuch pernicious defigns; and that which happened to a cheat, who was the cully of his own knaveries, will one day befal thee.

FABLE

# FABLE XXIII.

*Two young* MERCHANTS, *the one crafty, and the other without deceit.*

TWO young merchants once left their country to travel together upon the account of trade: the one was called Sharpwit, the other Simpleton. These two, in one of their first journeys, by accident found a bag full of money; on which said Sharpwit to his companion, Travelling, I believe, in truth, is very profitable, but it is also very very painful; therefore, brother, let us be contented with this money which fortune has thrown into our way, without fatiguing ourselves any more. Simpleton consenting to this, they left off their designs of travelling, and returned both to their lodging. Before they parted, Simpleton bethought himself of dividing what they had found, to the end they might be both at their own liberty. But, said Sharpwit, no, brother, believe me, it is much better to put it into a safe place, and every day to take something out of the stock for our occasions, without bringing the whole of our several fortunes into separate danger. To this Simpleton answered, that he very well approved of his proposal; and, accordingly, they hid the money, taking each of them only a small sum for their particular expences. The next day, however, Sharpwit went where the money lay, and, having taken it away, returned home. On the other hand, Simpleton thought not of going to the hoard while his little stock lasted; but, when he had expended all that he had, he went to Sharpwit's

wit's lodging, and meeting with him,. Come, said he, let us go together,- and take out such another sum as we took out before. Content, answered Sharpwit, for I have spent all my stock, and want money. So they went both together; but, when they came to the place where the money had been hid, behold the birds were flown. Sharpwit, on this, threw himself on the ground, tore his hair, rent his clothes, and, weeping to his companion, Why hast thou dealt so unkindly with thy friend? said he; for, nobody but you could take away the money, since nobody else knew where it was hid. It was in vain for Simpleton to swear he had not taken it away; the other still feigned to be assured of the contrary, and wickedly, not contented with robbing his brother of all he had, was for having him lose his life by false accusations, that he might be sure to have no more fear of his finding him out. What will not the wicked thirst after money compel us to! To conclude; at length they went both before a judge, before whom Sharpwit, after he had related the whole story, how they found the money, and how they agreed to hide it, accused Simpleton of having stolen it. The judge called presently for witnesses to prove the robbery; to which Sharpwit replied, I have no other witness but the tree that grows next the place; and, I hope God, who is just, will suffer the dumb tree to give testimony of the truth. The judge, admiring to hear the man talk at such a rate, resolved to see the issue of the business, and, accepting the tree for a witness, promised the next day to take a walk to the tree and examine it: and so the two merchants went home. In the mean time Sharpwit told his father the whole
story,

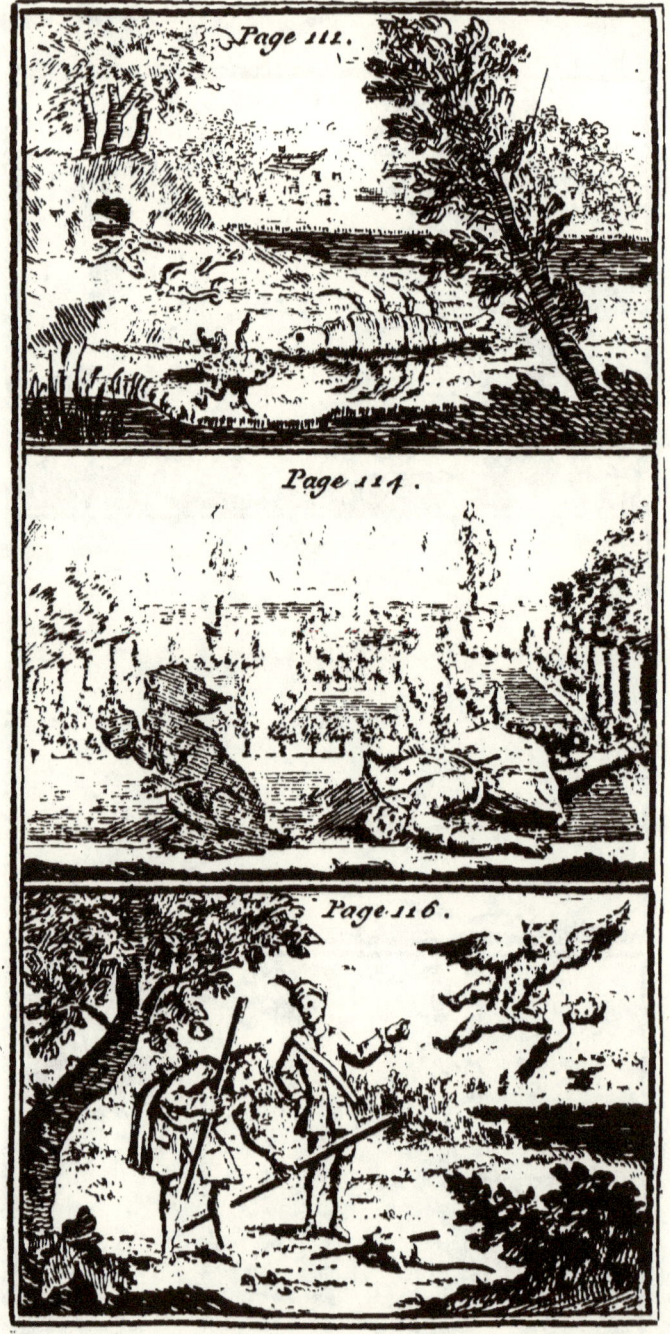

story, assuring him withal that he had no hope but in him when he took the tree for his evidence; and if you will but act your part, added he, we shall have the sum, which I have taken, to ourselves, and as much more from the party accused upon his condemnation, which will serve us very well the remainder of our days. His father, on this, asked him what he was to do: Why, sir, replied the son, you must go into the tree in the evening, and lie there all night, to the end that, when the judge comes betimes in the morning, you may give testimony according to the custom. O son! said the father, leave off these schemes of knavery, for, though thou mayest deceive men, thou canst never deceive the Almighty; and, I am afraid, thy fortune will have the same success with that of the frog.

## FABLE XXIV.

*The* FROG, *the* CRAY-FISH, *and the* SERPENT.

THERE was once a frog which had her habitation in the neighbourhood of the hole of a serpent, who, every time she had young ones, ate them up; this put her almost beside her wits; and, one day going to pay a visit to a cray-fish, that was one of her gossips, in the anguish of her heart she uttered many bitter imprecations against the serpent, and made her the confidant of her grievances. The cray-fish put her in good heart, assuring her, that a way might be be found out to rid her from such a pernicious neighbour. You will oblige me indeed, said the frog, if you will teach me that. Hark you then, replied the cray-fish, there is in such a place one of my comrades, who is very large, and indeed a monster among us; take you a sufficient number of little menows, and lay them all in a row from this cray-fish's hole to the serpent's lodging; for, the cray-fish that I tell you of will certainly snap them up all, one after another, till he comes where the serpent lies, who will come forth upon the noise, and then the cray-fish will devour him too. The frog followed this advice, and tasted the sweet pleasure of revenge. But, two days after, the cray-fish that had eaten the serpent, thinking to find more, went hunting in the same neighbourhood, and soon fell upon the place where the frog was now with another brood, and ate up not only all her young ones but herself also.

You see by this fable, concluded he, that deceivers are often deceived. Father, said the son, let me entreat you to leave off this idle discourse; we have no time now for talking, but must conclude either to earn the money, or go without it. Upon this, the old man, who was covetous enough, not able to dissuade his son, submitted, and went and hid himself in the tree. The next day, betimes in the morning, the judge made haste to the tree, accompanied by a great number of persons of wit and penetration, and a great croud of others that desired to be witnesses of this new way of accusation. After some ceremonies, the judge asked the tree, whether it were true that Simpleton had taken the money in dispute? Presently fently he heard a voice that anfwered, *Yes,—he is guilty of what he is accufed.* This fomewhat aftonifhed the judge at firft; but afterwards, furmifing that there might be fomebody in the tree, ordered all the boughs round about the tree to be heaped together and fet on fire. Upon which the poor old man, after he had endured the heat as long as he could, cried out, mercy, mercy; and, being then lifted out of the tree, confeffed the truth, made manifeft the innocence of Simpleton, and Sharpwit's wickednefs; for which he was punifhed as he deferved, while all the money was taken from the accufer and given to the party accufed.

I have recited this example to you, faid Kalila, to fhew you, that there is nothing like acting with uprightnefs and fincerity. You are to blame, faid Damna, to call wit by the name of knavery, and the care of a man's own interefts by the appellation of artifice: for my part, I am apt to think, that I have fhewed nothing but wit and judgement in my whole conduct. Thou art a wicked creature, cried Kalila, nor will I any longer liften to thee, or live with thee; thou teacheft fuch wicked maxims, that thofe who frequent thy company, I am afraid, will come to the fame end with a certain gardener, of whom I will tell thee a remarkable hiftory.

FABLE

# FABLE XXV.

## The GARDENER and the BEAR.

THERE was once, in the easterns parts of our country, a gardener who loved gardening to that degree, that he wholly absented himself from the company of men, to the end he might give himself up entirely to the care of his flowers and plants. He had neither wife nor children; and, from morning till night, he did nothing but work in his garden, so that it lay like a terrestrial paradise. At length, however, the good man grew weary of being alone, and took a resolution to leave his garden in search of good company.

As he was, soon after, walking at the foot of a mountain, he spied a bear, whose looks had in them nothing of the savage fierceness natural to that animal, but were mild and gentle. This bear was also weary of being alone, and came down from the mountain, for no other reason but to see whether he could meet with any one that would join society with him. So soon, therefore, as these two saw each other, they began to have a friendship for one another; and the gardener first accosted the bear, who, in return, made him a profound reverence. After some compliments passed between them, the gardener made the bear a sign to follow him; and, carrying him into his garden, regaled him with a world of very delicious fruit, which he had carefully preserved; so that at length they entered into a very strict friendship together; insomuch that, when

when the gardener was weary of working, and lay down to take a little nap, the bear, out of affection stayed all the while by him, and kept off the flies from his face. One day, as the gardener lay down to sleep at the foot of a tree, and the bear stood by, according to his custom, to drive away the flies, it happened that one of those insects did light upon the gardener's mouth, and, still as the bear drove it away from one side, it would light on the other; which put the bear into such a passion that he took up a great stone to kill it. It is true, he did kill the fly, but at the same time he broke out two or three of the gardener's teeth. Whence men of judgement observe, *That it is better to have a prudent enemy than an ignorant friend.*

This example shews, that we should take care whom we are concerned with; and I am of opinion that your society is no less dangerous than the company of the bear. This is an ill comparison, replied Damna, I hope I am not so ignorant but that I am able to distinguish between what is baneful and what is beneficial to my friend. Why, I know very well, indeed, replied Kalila, that your transgressions are not the failings of ignorance; but I know, too, that you can betray your friends, and that, when you do, it is not without long premeditation; witness the contrivance you made use of to set the lion and the poor ox together by the ears: but, after this, I cannot endure to hear you pretend to innocence. In short, you are like the man that would make his friend believe that rats eat iron.

FABLE

## FABLE XXVI.

*The* Merchant *and his* Friend.

A Certain merchant, said Kalila, pursuing her discourse, had once a great desire to make a long journey. Now, in regard that he was not very wealthy, It is requisite, said he to himself, that before my departure I should leave some part of my estate in the city, to the end that, if I meet with ill luck in my travels, I may have wherewithal to keep me at my return. To this purpose he delivered a great number of bars of iron, which were a principal part of his wealth, in trust to one of his friends, desiring him to keep them during his absence; and then, taking his leave, away he went. Some time after, having had but ill luck in his travels, he returned home; and the first thing he did was to go to his friend, and demand his iron: but his friend, who owed several sums of money, having sold the iron to pay his own debts, made him this answer: Truly, friend, said he, I put your iron into a room that was close locked, imagining it would have been there as secure as my own gold; but an accident has happened which nobody could have suspected; for, there was a rat in the room that ate it all up. The merchant, pretending ignorance, replied, it is a terrible misfortune to me indeed, but I know of old that rats love iron extremely; I have suffered by them many times before in the same manner, and therefore can the better bear my present affliction. This answer extremely
pleased

pleafed the friend, who was glad to hear the merchant fo well inclined to believe that the rats had eaten his iron; and, to remove all fufpicions, defired him to dine with him the next day. The merchant promifed he would; but in the mean time he met in the middle of the city one of his friend's children; the child he carried home, and locked up in a room. The next day he went to his friend, who feemed to be in great affliction, which he afked him the caufe of, as if he had been perfectly ignorant of what had happened. O my dear friend! anfwered the other, I beg you to excufe me, if you do not fee me fo chearful as otherwife I fhould be; I have loft one of my children;. I have had him cried by found of trumpet, but I know not what is become of him. Oh! replied the merchant, I am grieved to hear this, for, yefterday in the evening, as I parted hence, I faw an owl in the air with a child in his claws, but whether it were yours I cannot tell. Why, you moft foolifh and abfurd creature replied the friend, are you not afhamed to tell fuch an egregious lie? an owl, that weighs, at moft, not above two or three pounds, can he carry a boy that weighs above fifty? Why, replied the merchant, do you make fuch a wonder at that? as if, in a country where one rat can eat a hundred ton weight of iron, it were fuch a wonder for an owl to carry a child that weighs not above fifty pounds in all. The friend, upon this, found that the merchant was no fuch fool as he took him to be, begged his pardon for the cheat which he defigned to have put upon him, reftored him the value of his iron, and fo had his fon again.

This

This fable shews, continued Kalila, that these fine-spun deceits are not always successful; but, as to your principles, I can easily see that if you could be so unjust as to deceive the lion, to whom you were so much indebted for a thousand kindnesses, you will with much more confidence put your tricks upon those to whom you are less obliged. This is the reason why I think your company is dangerous.

While Damna and Kalila where thus confabulating together, the lion, whose passion was now over, made great lamentations for Cohotorbe, saying, that he began to be sensible of his loss, because of his extraordinary endowments. I know not, added he, whether I did ill or well in destroying him, or whether what was reported of him was true or false. Thus, musing for a while in a studious melancholy, at length he repented of having punished a subject, who might, for aught he knew, be innocent. Damna, observing that the lion was seized with remorse of conscience, left Kalila, and accosted the king with a most respectful humility: Sir, said he, what makes your majesty so pensive? consider, that here your enemy lies at your feet, and fix your eyes upon such an object with delight. When I think upon Cohotorbe's virtues, said the lion, I cannot but bemoan his loss. He was my support and my comfort, and it was by his prudent counsel that my people lived in repose. This indeed was once the case, replied Damna, but his revolt was therefore the more dangerous; and I am grieved to see your majesty bewail the death of an unfaithful subject. It is true he was profitable

fitable to the public; but, in regard he had a defign upon your perfon, you have done no more than what the wifeft have already advifed, which is to cut off a member that would prove the deftruction of the whole body. Thefe admonitions of Damna for the prefent gave the lion a little comfort: but, notwithftanding all, Cohotorbe's innocence crying continually afterwards in the monarch's breaft for vengeance, rouzed at laft fome thoughts in him, by which he found means to difcover the long chain of villanies Damna had been guilty of. *He that will reap wheat muft never fow barley. He only that does good actions, and thinks juft thoughts, will be happy in this world, and cannot fail of rewards and bleffings in the other.*

CHAP.

# CHAP. III.

*That the* WICKED *come to an ill end.*

I Have with great attention and delight, said Dabschelim, now heard the history of a sycophant, who, by his flatteries, deceived his prince, and was the cause that he wronged his minister: tell me therefore now, how the lion came to discover Damna's infidelities, and what was the end of this cunning and most wicked fox.

Kings, answered the old Bramin, are by no means to give any credit to the various reports that are whispered in their ears, till they understand whether the stories which they hear proceed from the lips of friends or enemies. It is with great delight that I have observed your majesty's attention to what I have been relating, and now shall joyfully proceed to give the account of those things which you yet desire to know. Some time after the lion had killed the ox, he was, as I have already observed, very much troubled in his mind; the reflections, that he continually made upon the good services which the ox had done him, plunged him into so deep a melancholy, that he abandoned the care of his dominions, and his court became a wilderness. He

talked

talked without intermission of Cohotorbe's rare endowments; and the good character which others gave him was the only consolation which his grief would admit. One night as he was wrapt up in discourse with the leopard concerning the virtues of the ox; Your majesty, said the leopard, too heavily afflicts yourself for a thing which it is impossible to remedy: and suffer me to remind your majesty, that he, that turmoils himself to seek what he cannot find, not only never acquires what he seeks, but, instead of that, loses what he has; as the fox once lost a hide, in hopes of getting a hen which he longed for. It is a remarkable story, and, if your majesty will give me permission, I will relate it to you.

## FABLE I.

*The* FOX, *the* WOLF, *and the* RAVEN.

A 'Certain fox, that was ranging about in search of food, found once a large piece of a raw hide, which some wild beast or other had let fall; he ate one part of it, and took the rest with a design to carry it to his hole; but, in his way, near a village, he spied several hens that were plump and fat, which a certain boy, set to watch them, had always in his eye. These dainties set the fox's teeth watering to that degree that he left his raw hide, which he was sure of, to get one of these delicate morsels. At the same instant came a wolf up to him, and asked him what

what he gazed after with so much earnestness.
Those hens that you see yonder, answered the
fox; I would fain have one of them for my second course. You will only lose your time, replied the wolf, in attempting it; they are guarded by so vigilant a servant that it is impossible for
you to get near them without running a manifest hazard. Take my advice therefore, content
yourself with a piece of raw hide, for fear you
meet with the same hard fortune that once befel
the ass, who, while he was looking after his tail,
lost his ears.

## FABLE II.

### The Ass and the Gardener.

A Certain ass, continued he, had once by some
accident lost his tail, which was a grievous
affliction to him; and, as he was every where seeking after it, being fool enough to think he could
set it on again, he passed through a meadow, and
afterwards got into a garden. The gardener seeing him, and not able to endure the mischief he
was doing in trampling down his garden, fell into a violent rage, ran to the ass, and, never standing on the ceremony of a pillory, cut of both his
ears, and beat him out of the ground. Thus,
the ass, who bemoaned the loss of his tail, was
in far greater affliction when he saw himself
without ears: and believe me, that, in general,
whoever he be, that takes not reason for his
guide,

guide, wanders about, and at length falls into precipices.

The fox, however, was still eagerly importuned by his extraordinary longing after a tit-bit: What come you hither for, said he to the wolf, to trouble me with your morals and your fables? I will let you see, that he who has courage scorns the terror of such examples, and dares do any thing. So saying, he advanced slily toward the hens, leaving his piece of raw hide; and the wolf, finding that his admonitions would do no good, went about his business. In the mean time the fox crept softly toward his feathered prey; but the boy, perceiving his thievish intention, threw a large stone so luckily at him, that he hit him on the foot. The poor fox, afraid lest the boy should reach his pate next time, returned with much more haste than he came, resolving to be contented with his piece of raw hide. But, alas! that was gone too;. for, a raven coming by at the same time, had carried it away; and the fox could now have torn his own flesh for madness.

You see, sir, pursued the leopard, by these stories, the misfortunes that attend rash and inconsiderate enterprizes; and permit me to add, that your majesty ought never to despair, nor abandon the government of your dominions for the loss of one subject. On this the lion for a while stood mute, but then recovering his speech, You say true, said he, but, if I do not this, I would at least ease my troubled mind, and strongly revenge Cohotorbe's death if I could find that he had been unjustly accused. This is a just and a noble intent,

tent, replied the leopard; but, sir, desponding is not the way to attain your end: you must carefully examine whether the complaints, that were brought you of his miscarriages, were true or not. If he was guilty, he has been deservedly punished; if not, the accuser ought to feel your severity. Then, said the lion to the leopard, I appoint thee my searcher of the truth on this occasion, and entreat thee to do all thou canst to find it out.

Now, in regard it was by this time late, the leopard, for the present, took his leave of the lion: but in his way to his lodging, passing by Kalila and Damna's apartment, he thought he heard them discoursing together. The leopard had long suspected Damna to be no less wicked than indeed he was, and his curiosity therefore led him to go near and listen. Kalila, as fortune would have it, was at this very time upbraiding her husband with his perfidiousness, his dissimulation, and all the artifices he had made use of to ruin Cohotorbe. The leopard, fully informed by her reproaches of Damna's treasons, went immediately away to the lion's mother, to whom he related what he had heard; and she presently hasted to her son, crying to him, You have reason indeed to be afflicted for the loss of Cohotorbe, your favourite; for, he died innocent. What proof have you of this? demanded the lion eagerly. Pardon me, answered the mother, if I am not so hasty to reveal a secret which may, if too suddenly related to you, inflame your anger to too high a degree, and prejudice the person that has intrusted me. But I beseech you listen to this fable.

FABLE

# FABLE III.

## The PRINCE and his MINISTER.

THERE was once a prince who was very much famed throughout all these countries; he was a great conqueror, and was potent, rich, and just. One day, as he was hunting, said he to his minister, put on thy best speed, I will run my horse against thine, that we may see which is the swiftest: I have a long time had a strange desire to make this trial. The minister, in obedience to his master, put on his horse, and rode full speed, and the king followed him. But, when they were got a great distance from the grandees and nobles that accompanied them, the king, stopping his horse, said to his minister, I had no other design in this but to bring thee to a place where we might be alone; for I have a secret to impart to thee, having found thee more faithful than any other of my servants. I have a jealousy that the prince, my brother, is framing some contrivance against my person, and, for that reason, I have made choice of thee to prevent him; but be discreet. The minister on this swore he would be true to him; and, when they had thus agreed, they staid till the company overtook them, who were in great trouble for the king's person. The minister, however, notwithstanding his promises to the king, upon the first opportunity he had to speak with the king's brother, disclosed to him the design that was brewing to take away his life. And this obliged the young prince to thank him for his information, promise him great rewards,

wards, and take some precautions in regard to his own safety.

Some few days after, the king died, and his brother succeeded him: but, when the minister, who had done him this signal service, expected now some great preferment, the first thing he did, after he was advanced to the throne, was to order him to be put to death. The poor wretch, immediately upbraided him with the service he had done him. Is this, said he, the recompence for my friendship to you? this the reward which you promised me? Yes, answered the new king, whoever reveals the secrets of his prince deserves no less than death: and, since thou hast committed so foul a crime, thou deservest to die. Thou betrayedst a king who put his confidence in thee, and who loved thee above all his court, how is it possible therefore for me to trust thee in my service? It was in vain for the minister to allege any reasons in his own justification, they would not be heard, nor could he escape the stroke of the executioner.

You see by this fable, son, continued the old lioness, that secrets are not to be disclosed. But, my dear mother, answered the king, he, that entrusted you with this secret, desires that it should be made known, seeing he is the first that makes the discovery: for, if he could not keep it himself, how could he desire another to be more reserved? Let me conjure you, continued he, if what you have to say be true, put me out of my pain. The mother seeing herself so hardly prest; then, said she, I must inform you of a criminal unworthy of pardon; for, though it be the saying of wise men, that a king ought to be merciful, yet there are
certain

certain crimes that never ought to be forgiven. It is Damna I mean, purfued the matron lionefs, who, by his falfe infinuatious, wrought Cohotorbe's fall. And having fo faid, fhe retired, leaving the lion in a deep aftonifhment. Some time he pondered with himfelf on this difcovery, and afterwards fummoned an affembly of the whole court. Damna taking umbrage at this (as guilty confciences always make people cowards) comes to one of the king's favourites, and afks him if he knew the reafon of the lion's calling fuch an affembly? Which the lion's mother overhearing, Yes, faid fhe, it is to pronounce thy death ; for thy artifice and ·juggling politics are now, though too late, difcovered. Madam, anfwered Damna, they who render themfelves worthy of efteem and honour at court by their virtues never fail of enemies. Oh! that we, added he, would act no otherwife than as the Almighty acts in regard to us; for, he gives to every one according to his defert; but we, on the other fide, frequently punifh thofe who were worthy of reward, and as often cherifh thofe that deferve our indignation. How much was I to blame to quit my folitude, merely to confecrate my life to the king's fervice, to meet with this reward. Whoever, continued he, diffatisfied with what he has, prefers the fervice of princes before his duty to his Creator, will be fure, -I find, early or late to repent in vain. This your ladyfhip may fee by the following ftory.

G 4  FABLE

## FABLE IV.

*A* HERMIT *who quitted the desert to live at court.*

THERE was once, in a remote part of his majesty's (my hitherto most gracious master's) dominions, a certain hermit, who had renounced the pleasures of the world, and led a very austere life in a wilderness. His virtue, in a small time, made such a noise in the world, that an infinite number of people flocked every day to consult him upon several different matters. The fame of this hermit's wisdom and virtue spread every day more and more. The king of the country, who was very devout, and who loved all virtuous and worthy men, no sooner understood that there was in his kingdom a person of so much knowledge and goodness, but he rode to see him, made him a noble present, and desired that he might hear some of his learned and virtuous exhortations. On this desire of the monarch the hermit began, and laid before him a most glorious scene of true knowledge. Sir, said he, the almighty Governor of the universe has two habitations, the one perishable, which is the world, the other eternal, which is the abode of the blessed hereafter. It is not for your majesty, therefore, to dote upon the felicities of the earth; you ought to aspire to those eternal treasures, the meanest part of which is of a nobler value than all the principalities of the world. Try then, sacred sir, with earnestness, to attain the possession of those eternal blessings,

and

and you shall not lose the reward of your endeavours. The monarch, on this, demanded by what assiduities they might be acquired. By a series of virtuous actions alone, replied the hermit; particularly by relieving the poor and succouring the distressed; for, of this be ever mindful: all princes, that desire to enjoy eternal repose, must labour to give temporal tranquillity to their subjects.

The king was so taken with this discourse, that he took up a resolution to spend some hours with this good hermit every day, and so, for the present, returned to his palace. Long continued he every day his visits to this oracle of truth: among the rest, one day, as the king and the hermit were together in the hermitage, they saw a confused multitude of people thronging toward them, and rending the air with loud cries of Justice, justice. The hermit went to the door of the cave, and, bidding them draw near, examined them; and, having understood their differences, made a quick and peaceful accommodation between them, sending them away all praying for a thousand blessings on him. The king, upon this, admiring the hermit's prudence and dispatch, desired him that he would favour him so far as, for the sake of the public good, sometimes to leave his tranquil abode for a few hours, and be present in his councils. The hermit readily agreed to this, believing he might be beneficial to the poor; and, after this, was frequently in those assemblies; and the king ever pronounced his decrees according to his judgement, insomuch that, at length he became so necessary, that nothing was done in the kingdom without his advice.

The hermit, now beginning to find that men made their addresses to him, began to forget his de-

determined solitude and humility, and soon took upon him the rank and quality of chief minister. To which end he provided himself with a rich livery and a numerous train. He now forgot his austerities, his penances, and his prayers, and, looking upon himself as one that would be greatly missed in the government, took great care of his own person, lay soft, and fed upon the most exquisite dainties: and the king, who was very well satisfied with the hermit, let him do as he pleased, and, in short, discharged upon his shoulders the whole burden of his care.

One day another hermit, a friend to him that lived at court, coming to visit his brother, with whom he had frequently spent whole nights in prayer and whole days in fasting and penitence, was astonished to see him arrayed in costly habits, and environed with a great number of servants: reserving his patience, however, till night locked up all the court in dark retirement; when all was hushed, accosting the courtier-hermit in the most pathetic manner, O my dear friend, said he, in what a condition do I find you? what a strange alteration is this? and what is now become of all the sanctity that you used to pretend to? The court-hermit would fain have excused himself, by saying, That he was constrained to keep so great a train: but his brother, who was a person of wit and judgement, said, these excuses are the dictates of sensuality; I see that wealth and preferments have enchanted your devotion. What demon has put you out of conceit with your praying-life? and why, forgetting the duties of a retired station, do you here prefer noise before silence, and tumult before ease? Think not,

not, answered the court-hermit, that the business of the court is any hindrance to me from continuing my devotions; no, brother, I continue them with more than wonted fervour, and hourly return my humble thanks to heaven for placing me in a station where I may do good to the world. You deceive yourself, replied the brother-hermit, to think that your prayers can be heard, while you are environed with the cares and pomps of the world, as they were when holy and heavenly duties took up all your time; no, no, I adjure you, therefore, take my advice, break these chains of gold that bind you to the court, and return to your desert; otherwise, be assured, you will, at last, meet with the cruel destiny of the blind man, who despised the counsel of his friend.

## FABLE V.

*The* BLIND MAN *who travelled with one of his* FRIENDS.

THERE were once, continued he, two men that travelled together, one of which was blind. These two companions, being in the course of their journey one time surprized by night upon the road, entered into a meadow, there to rest themselves till morning; and, as soon as day appeared, they rose, got on horseback, and continued their journey. Now, the blind man, instead of his whip, as ill fate would have it, had picked up a serpent that was stiff with cold; but having

having it in his hand, as it grew a little warm, he felt it somewhat softer than his whip, which pleased him very much; he thought he had gained by the change, and therefore never minded the loss. In this manner he travelled some time; but, when the sun began to appear and illuminate the world, his companion perceived the serpent, and with loud cries, Friend, said he, you have taken up a serpent instead of your whip; throw it out of your hand, before you feel the mortal caresses of the venomous animal. But the blind man, no less blind in his intellects than his body, believing that his friend had only jested with him to get away his whip, What! said he, do you envy my good luck? I lost my whip that was worth nothing, and here my kind fortune has sent me a new one. Pray do not take me for such a changeling but that I can distinguish a serpent from a whip. With that his friend replied, Companion, I am obliged by the laws of friendship and humanity to inform you of your danger; and therefore let me again assure you of your error, and conjure you, if you love your life, throw away the serpent. To which the blind man, more exasperated than persuaded, Why do you take all these pains to cheat me, and press me thus to throw away a thing, which you intend, as soon as I have done so, to pick up yourself? His companion, grieved at his obstinacy, intreated him to be persuaded of the truth, swore he had no such design, and protested to him that what he held in his hand was a real and poisonous serpent. But neither oaths nor protestations could prevail, the blind man would not alter his resolution. The sun, by this time, began to grow high;

high, and his beams having warmed the ferpent by degrees, he began to crawl up the blind man's arm, which he immediately after bit in fuch a venomous manner, that he gave him his death's wound.

This example teaches us, brother, continued the pious hermit, that we ought to diftruft our fenfes, and that it is a difficult tafk to mafter them, when we are in poffeffion of the thing that flatters our fancy.

This appofite fable, and judicious admonition, awaked the court-hermit from his pleafing dream; he opened his eyes, and furveyed the hazards that he ran at court; and, bewailing the time which be had vainly fpent in the fervice of the world, he paffed the night in fighs and tears. His friend conftantly attended him, and rejoiced he had made him a convert; but, alas, day being come, the new honours that were done him deftroyed all his repentance. At this melancholy fight, the pious ftranger, with tears in his eyes, and many prayers for his loft brother, as he accounted him, took his leave of the court and retired to his cell. On the other hand, the courtier began to thruft himfelf into all manner of bufinefs, and foon became unjuft, like the people of the world. One day, in the hurry of his affairs, he rafhly and inconfiderately condemned to death a perfon, who, according to the laws and cuftoms of the country, ought not to have fuffered capital puifhment. After the execution of the fentence, his confcience teazed him with reproaches that troubled his repofe for fome time; and, at length, the heirs of the perfon whom he had

had unjuftly condemned, with great difficulty, obtained leave of the king to inform againft the hermit, whom they accufed of injuftice and oppreffion; and the council, after mature debate upon the informations, ordered that the hermit fhould fuffer the fame punifhment which he had inflicted upon the perfon deceafed. The hermit made ufe of all his credit and his riches to fave his life. But all availed not, and the decree of the council was executed.

I muft confefs, faid Damna, that, according to this example, I ought, long fince, to have been punifhed for having quitted my folitude to ferve the king; notwithftanding that I can fafely appeal to heaven, that I am guilty of no crime againft any perfon yet.

Damna here gave over fpeaking, and his eloquence was admired by all the court. Different opinions were formed of him by the different perfons prefent. And as for the lion, he held down his head, turmoiled with fo many various thoughts that he knew not what to refolve, nor what anfwer to give. While the lion, however, was in this dilemma, and all the courtiers kept filence, a certain creature, called Siagoufch, who was one of the moft faithful fervants the king had, ftept forward, and fpoke to this effect:

O thou moft wicked wretch, all the reproaches, which thou throweft upon thofe that ferve kings, turn only to thy own fhame; for, befides that it does no way belong to thee to enter into thefe affairs, know that an hour of fervice done to the king is worth a hundred years of prayer. Many perfons of merit have we feen, that have quitted their little cells

to

to go to court, where, serving princes, they have eased the people, and secured them from tyrannical oppressions. The fable which I am going to tell you may serve for a proof of what I say.

---

## FABLE VI.

*A religious* DOCTOR *and a* DERVISE.

THERE once lived in a certain city of Persia, an ancient religious doctor, who spent his life wholly in his proper calling, the inculcating true notions of virtue, piety, and religion, into persons of all ranks. This excellent man had an established reputation, throughout the kingdom, of being a very learned and virtuous man. He was called Rouchan Zamir, that is to say, *clear conscience*. A dervise, of great fame once, pushed on by the motions of an extraordinary devotion, parted from Mauralnachos, a province of Tartary, to visit this religious doctor, and to consult him upon some difficult questions. After much fatigue he arrived at the habitation of our doctor: the doctor, himself, however, was not within, but a person, that he kept as his constant companion, was there, who, observing that the dervise was weary, desired him to rest himself; adding, that this was the hour at which the doctor usually returned from court, whither he went every day. Here all was at once destroyed; for, when the dervise heard that the religious doctor, Clear Conscience, intermeddled with state affairs, Oh! cried he, how sorry I am to have come so far and lost my time and labour! for, I am very well assured that

that there is nothing to be learned from a man that frequents courts. With these words, he departed from the place with a very ill opinion of the religious doctor. Now it happened, that the captain of the watch was searching about that day for a notorious robber, who had made his escape the night before; and the king had threatened to put him to death if he did not find him again. This captain, meeting the dervise, seized him instead of the offender whom he sought for, and, without examining him, hurried him away immediately to execution. It was in vain for the dervise to swear himself an honest man, his tale would not be heard, and already the hangman had his knife ready to take off his head, when our religious doctor, returning from court, saw the dervise in the hands of the executioner. The doctor immediately ordered him to be untied, affirming him to be one of his brethren, and that it was impossible he should have committed the crime of which he was accused. The executioner made a profound reverence to the doctor, fell upon his knee, and kissed his hand, and unbound the dervise, who accompanied the doctor to his habitation. As they were going on, the doctor entered on the occasion of his present manner of life with his released friend. Be not surprized, said he, that I spend the greatest part of my time at court; I live not after this manner for the sake of the vanities of the world; these, believe me, brother, I have no taste for; no, it is for nobler ends that I attend a court. Injustice and oppression too often reign there; these I spend my labours to prevent, and devote my life to what I abhor, that I may be able to rescue the

stranger

stranger from destruction, make the distressed be relieved, and to deliver from death the innocent, such as you are. The dervise, on this, acknowledging that he had made a most rash and wicked judgement, told the doctor, that, from that time forward, he would never blame those that went to court for good purposes.

By this example, added Siagoufch, we see that the greatest observers of the law and truest followers of virtue are not always banished from the court. It is true, replied Damna, that sometimes most virtuous men do live at court; but it is not till after they have implored the succour of heaven, because they know full well, that, unless heaven particularly protect them, they must, of necessity, ruin themselves. Besides, these people never come to court till they have absolutely laid aside all private interests, which is the most dangerous rock that they can split upon. I confess, that, with a mind so free from interest, a man may embrace all sorts of conditions. But we, alas! that are not endowed with such a sublime virtue, how shall we, with safety to ourselves, exercise an employment so dangerous, unless we have the good fortune also to serve just and penetrating princes, who, being able to distinguish faithful from wicked servants, reward and punish them according to the rules of justice?

On this, the mother of the lion, rising from her seat, with a look of conscious knowledge and disdain, said, Damna, we all allow the truth of what you have been saying; but, know you too, that this assembly sits not here but to upbraid thee for thy perfidy to the best of princes, and

knew not what to resolve. After much deliberation, we must refer this cause, said he, to a select number of judges; for, it is my pleasure that this affair be thoroughly and carefully examined. Most justly ordained, cried Damna; for, they who judge with precipitation commonly judge amiss. Most gladly I submit myself to such a tribunal, and humbly adore your majesty's wisdom and goodness for appointing it. My innocence, I doubt not, in time, will clear itself, though a hasty judgement might unknowingly have pronounced me guilty: nothing ought to be decided in things of consequence, without having a perfect knowledge of the whole affair, otherwise we may be deluded as the woman was, whose adventure, with your majesty's permission, I will relate to this august assembly.

## FABLE VII.

### The MERCHANT'S WIFE and the PAINTER.

A Merchant of the city of Catchemir had once a very beautiful wife, who loved and was beloved by a painter who excelled in his art. These two lovers doated on each other to that degree, that they neglected no possible opportunity to be in each other's company. One day, said the mistress to her gallant, I find that, when you would speak to me, you are constrained to make a great many troublesome signs, as counterfeiting your voice, whistling, coughing, and the like; but I would have us learn some way to spare all these pains. Cannot you think of some invention that may serve us by way of a signal? Yes, replied the painter, I have often had it in my thoughts, and I will now do it; I will paint two masks, the whiteness of one of which shall surpass the brightness of a star, and the blackness of the other shall outvie the locks of a moor. When you see me come forth with one or the other of these masks, you will know what they signify. The painter's apprentice, who was no less in love with the woman than his master, being in the next room, heard this agreement between the two lovers, and resolved to make his own advantage of it. Accordingly, soon after this, one day, when his master was gone to draw some lady's picture in the city, he took the mask of assignation, and walked before the house of the merchant's wife, who stood, as good fortune would have it, at that very time watching at the window. The lady no sooner saw the mask of joy, but, without considering either the bearer's appearance or gait, she came down and admitted him immediately to all the familiarities she was used to accommodate his master with. After all was over, the apprentice returned home, and put the mask where he had it. A very little while after this, the painter, being come back, took out the mask, and went to look out for his mistress. The lady very much wondered to see the mask again so soon; but, however with open arms, ran to meet her joy. She scarce opened her mouth, however, before she unfortunately asked him the reason of his quick return. The painter, on this, smelling a rat, said not a word more, but flung from her in a passion, flew to his apprentice, and made him pay dear for the pleasure he had tasted: then,

reflecting

reflecting upon the eafy condefcenfion of the merchant's wife to fatisfy the defires of his fervant, he broke off all familiarity with her. Now, if the woman had not concluded too haftily on feeing the mafk, and yielded to the extafies of the apprentice, fhe had not loft fo paffionate, though criminal, a lover.

The lion's mother obferving that her fon gave ear to Damna with delight, was afraid left the fubtle fox fhould by his eloquence put a ftop to the courfe of juftice. Son, therefore, faid fhe to the lion, my mind forebodes to me that you will believe Damna innocent, and that you look upon all thofe that have accufed him as liars. I never thought, continued fhe, that a king, who is looked upon to be the moft juft of princes, could fuffer himfelf to be thus feduced by the fair words and gloffing infinuations of a capital offender, who is endeavouring at nothing, by all thefe fine ftories, but to deceive you, and to efcape the rigour of the law. So faying, fhe rofe up in a great paffion, and retired to her own apartment; and the lion, partly to pacify his mother, and partly, becaufe he began to think Damna guilty, ordered him to be committed to a clofe prifon.

When the room was clear, his mother returned, and addreffing herfelf to her fon; Son, faid fhe, think me not invidious in my nature for thus pufhing on the fate of this offender: it is with reluctance that I have done it, but juftice to yourfelf, and to the departed innocent Cohotorbe, requires it. Guilty he unqueftionably is, in the higheft degree; but yet, when I recollect all circumftances of his life, I cannot conceive how a perfon of fo much underftanding came to fuffer

him-

himself to be tempted to so great a crime. Certainly, answered the king, this has been the effect of envy in him, that has made him commit so foul a piece of treachery; which is a vice able to destroy the cunningest minds. Envy, pursued he, is a vice that keeps the thoughts in a perpetual motion, and torments us with continual disquiet. Nay, so strangely detestable a passion is this, that there are some who bear a grudge even to those that do them good. This you may know by the following example.

## FABLE VIII.

*Three envious persons who found money.*

THREE men once were travelling the same road, and soon by that means became acquainted. As they were journeying on, said the eldest to the rest, pray tell me, fellow-travellers, why you leave your settled homes to wander in foreign countries. I have quitted my native soil, answered one, because I could not not endure the sight of some people whom I hated worse than death: and this hatred of mine, I must confess, was not founded on any injury done me by them, but arose from my own temper, which, I own it, cannot endure to see another happy. Few words will give you my answer, replied the second; for, the same distemper torments my breast, and sends me rambling about the world. Friends, replied the eldest, then let us all embrace; for, I find we are all three troubled with
the

the same disease. On these reciprocal confessions they soon became acquainted, and, being of the same humour, immediately closed in an union together. One day, as they travelled through a certain deep hollow way, they spied a bag of money, which some traveller had dropped in the road. Presently they alighted, all three, and cried one to another, let us share this money and return home again, where we may be merry and enjoy ourselves. But this they only said in dissimulation; for, every one being unwilling that his companion should have the least benefit, they were truly each of them at a stand, whether it were not best to go on without meddling with the bag, to the end the rest might do the same; being well contented not to be happy themselves lest another should be so also. In conclusion, they stopt a whole day and night in the same place to consider what they should do. At the end of which time the king of the country riding out hunting with all his court, the chace led him into this place. He rode up to the three men, and asked them what they did with the money that lay on the ground? and, being thus surprized, and dreading some ill consequence if they equivocated, they all frankly told the truth. Sir, said they, we are all three turmoiled with the same passion, which is envy: this passion has forced us to quit our native country, and still keeps us company wherever we go; and a great act of kindness would it be in any one, if it were possible, that he would cure us of this accursed passion, which, though we cannot but carry it in our bosoms, yet we hate and abhor. Well, said the king, I will be your doctor; but, before

I

I can do any thing, it is requisite that everyone of you should inform me truly in what degree this passion prevails over him, to the end that I may apply a remedy in proper proportion of strength. My envy, alas! said the first, has got such a head, that I cannot endure to do good to any man living. You are an honest man in comparison to me, cried the second; for, I am so far from doing good to another myself, that I mortally hate that any body else should do another man good. Said the third, you both are children in this passion to me; neither of you possess the quality of envy in a degree to be compared with me; for I not only cannot endure to oblige, nor to see any other person obliged, but I even hate that any body should do myself a kindness. The king was so astonished to hear them talk at this rate, that he knew not what to answer. At length, after he had considered some time, Monsters, and not men, that ye are, said he, you deserve not that I should let you have the money, but punishment, if that can be, adequate to your tempers. At the same time he commanded the bag to be taken from them, and condemned them to punishments they justly merited. He that could not endure to do good was sent into the desert, barefoot and without provision. He, that could not endure to see good done to another, had his head chopped off, because he was unworthy to live, as being one that loved nothing but mischief. And lastly, as for him that could not endure any good to be done to himself, his life was spared, in regard his torment was only to himself; and he was put into a quarter of the kingdom where the people were of all others famous for being the best-natured, and the

most

most addicted to the performance of good deeds and charitable actions. The goodness of these people, and the favours they conferred upon him from day to day, soon became such torment to his soul, that he died in the utmost anguish.

By this history, continued the lion, you see what envy is; that it is of all vices the most abominable, and most to be expelled out of all human society. Most true, replied the mother, and it is for that very reason that Damna ought to be put to death, since he is attainted of so dangerous a vice. If he be guilty, replied the lion, he shall perish; but that I am not yet well assured of, but have resolved to be before he is condemned.

While matters were thus carrying on at court, however, Damna's wife, moved with compassion, went to see him in his prison, and read him this curtain-lecture. Did I not tell you, said she, that it behoved you to take care of going on with the execution of your enterprize; and that people of judgement and discretion never begin a business till they have warily considered what will be the issue of it? A tree is never to be planted, spouse, continued she, before we know what fruit it will produce. While Kalila was thus upbraiding Damna, there was in the prison a bear, of whom they were not aware, and who, having overheard them, resolved to make use of what his ears had furnished him withal, as occasion should direct him.

The next day, betimes in the morning, the council met again; where, after every one had taken his place, the mother of the lion thus began.

gan. Let me remind your majesty, said she, that we ought no more to delay the punishment of a capital offender than to hurry on the condemnation of the innocent; and that a king, that forbears the punishment of a malefactor, is guilty of no less a crime than if he had been a confederate with him. The old lady spoke this with much earnestness; and the lion, considering that she spoke nothing but reason, commanded that Damna should be immediately brought to his trial. On this, the chief justice, rising from his seat, made the accustomed speech on such occasions, and desired the several members of the council to speak, and give their opinion freely, boldly, and honestly, in this matter; saying, withal, that it would produce three great advantages. First, that truth would be found out, and justice done. Secondly, that wicked men and traitors would be punished. And, thirdly, that the kingdom would be cleared of knaves and impostors, who, by their artifices, troubled the repose of it. But notwithstanding the eloquence of the judge, as nobody then present knew the depth of the business, none opened their mouths to speak. This gave Damna an occasion to defend himself with so much the greater confidence and intrepidity: Sir, said he, rising slowly from his seat, and making a profound reverence to his majesty and the court, had I committed the crime of which I stand accused, I might draw some colour of advantage from the general silence; but I find myself so innocent, that I wait with indifference the end of this assembly. Nevertheless, I must needs say this, that, seeing nobody has been pleased to deliver his sentiments upon this affair, it is a certain

tain sign that all believe me innocent. Let me not, sacred sir, be blamed for speaking in my own justification: I am to be excused in that, since it is lawful for every one to defend himself. Therefore, said he, pursuing his discourse, I beseech all this illustrious company to say in the king's presence whatever they know concerning me; but let me caution them at the same time to have a care of affirming any thing but what is true, lest they find themselves involved in what befel the ignorant physician; of whom, with your majesty's permission, I will relate the fable.

## FABLE IX.

### *The* IGNORANT PHYSICIAN.

THERE was once, in a remote part of the east, a man who was altogether void of knowledge and experience, yet presumed to call himself a physician. He was so ignorant, notwithstanding, that he knew not the cholic from the dropsy, nor could he distinguish rhubarb from bezoar. He never visited a patient twice, for his first coming always killed him. On the other hand, there was in the same province another physician of such learning and ability, that he cured the most desperate diseases by the virtue of the several herbs of the country, of which he had a perfect knowledge. Now this learned man became blind, and, not being able to visit his patients, at length retired into a desart, there to live at his ease. The ignorant physician no sooner understood

understood that the only man he looked upon with an envious eye was retired out of the way, but he began boldly to display his ignorance, under the opinion of manifesting his knowledge. One day the king of the country's daughter fell sick; upon which the knowing physician was sent for, because that, besides that he had already served the court, people were convinced that he was much more able than he that went about to set himself up in this pompous manner. The learned physician being in the princess's chamber, and understanding the nature of her disease, ordered her to take a certain pill composed of such ingredients as he prescribed. Presently they asked him, where such and such drugs were to be had. Formerly, answered the physician, I have seen them in such and such boxes in the king's treasury; but what confusion there may have been since among those boxes I know not. Upon this the ignorant physician pretended that he knew the drugs very well, and that he also knew where to find and how to make use of them. Go then, said the king, to my treasury, and take what is requisite. Away went the ignorant physician, and fell to searching for the box; but, because many of the boxes were alike, and for that he knew not the drugs when he saw them, he knew not what to determine. On the whole, however, he rather chose, in the puzzle of his judgement, to take a box at a venture than to acknowledge his ignorance. But he never considered, that they who meddle with what they understand not are generally constrained to an early repentance; for, in the box which he had picked out, there was a most exquisite poison, of which he made his pills,

and

and which he caufed the princefs to take, who died immediately after. On which the king commanded the ignorant phyfician to be apprehended, and condemned him to death.

This example, purfued Damna, teaches us, that no man ought to fay or do a thing which he underftands not. A man may, however, perceive by your phyfiognomy, faid one of the affiftants, interrupting him, notwithftanding thefe fine fpeeches, that you are a fly companion, one that can talk better than you can act, and therefore I pronounce that there is little heed to be given to what you fay. The judge on this afked him that fpoke laft, what proof he could produce of the certainty of what he averred. Phyfiognomifts, anfwered he, obferve, that they who have their eye-brows parted, the left eye bleared, and bigger than the right, the nofe turned toward the left fide, and who, counterfeiting your hypocrites, caft their eyes always toward the ground, are generally traitors and fycophants; and therefore, Damna having all thefe marks, from what I know of the art, I thought I might fafely give that character of him which I have done, without injury to truth. Your art may fail you, replied Damna; for, it is our Creator alone who forms us as he pleafes, and gives us fuch a phyfiognomy as he thinks fitting, and for what purpofes he beft knows: and permit me to add, that, if what you fay were true, and every man carried written in his forehead what he had in his heart, the wicked might certainly be diftinguifhed from the righteous at fight, and there would be no need of judges and witneffes to determine the difputes and differences that arife in civil society. In like manner it would be unjust to put some to their oaths, and others to the rack, to discover the truth, because it might be evidently seen. And, if the marks you have mentioned imposed a necessity upon those that bear them to act amiss, would it not be palpable injustice to punish the wicked, since they are not free in their own actions? We must then conclude, according to this maxim, that if I were the cause of Cohotorbe's death, I am not to be punished for it, since I am not master of my actions, but was forced to it by the marks which I bear. You see by this way of arguing, therefore, that your inferences are false. Damna having thus stopt the assistant's mouth, nobody durst adventure to say any thing more, which forced the judge to send him back to prison, and left the king yet undetermined what to think of him.

Damna, being returned to his prison, was about to have sent a messenger to Kalila to come to him, when a brother fox, that was in the room by accident spared him that trouble, by informing him of Kalila's death, who died the day before for grief to see her husband intangled in such an unfortunate affair.

The news of Kalila's death touched Damna so to the quick, that, like one who cared not to live any longer, he seemed to be altogether comfortless. Upon which the fox endeavoured to chear him up, telling him, that, if he had lost a dear and loving wife, he might, however, if he pleased to try him, find in him a zealous and a faithful friend. Damna, on this, knowing he had no friend left that he could trust, and for that the

*fox*

fox so frankly proffered him his service, accepted his kindness. I beseech you then, said Damna, go to the court, and give me a faithful account of what people say of me: this is the first proof of friendship which I desire of you.

Most willingly, answered the fox; and, immediately taking his leave, he went to the court, to see what observations he could make.

The next morning, by break of day, the lion's mother went to her son, and asked him what he had determined to do with Damna. He is still in prison, answered the king, and I can find nothing proved upon him yet, nor know I what to do about him. What a deal of difficulty is here, replied the mother, to condemn a traitor and a villain, who deserves more punishments than you can inflict; and yet I am afraid, when all is done, will escape by his dexterity and cunning. I cannot blame you for being discontented with these delays, replied the king, for I also am so, but know not how to help myself; and, if you please to be present at his next examination yourself, I will order it immediately, and you shall see what will be resolved upon. Which said, he ordered Damna to be sent for, that the business might be brought to a conclusion. The king's orders were obeyed; and, the prisoner being brought to the bar, the chief justice put the same question as the day before, Whether any body had any thing to say against Damna? but nobody said a word; which Damna observing, I am glad to see, said he, that in your majesty's court there is not a single villain; few sovereign princes can say as much: but here is a proof of the truth of it before us, in that there is nobody

here

here who will bear false witness, though it be wished by every one that something were said: and, in other courts, it were well if the same honour and honesty were kept up: and let me advise all from the villany of bearing false witness, for their own sakes, and for fear of exposing themselves to the punishment which the falconer once incurred, for having given a false testimony.

---

## FABLE X.

### *The* virtuous WOMAN *and the* young FALCONER.

A Very honest and rich merchant had once a wife no less modest than beautiful: among the rest of his servants this merchant had also a young lad that was very vicious; but he could not find in his heart to put him away, because he was a good falconer, and the merchant greatly delighted in this diversion. Now, in regard it is the custom of the eastern people to keep their women very private, this lad for a long time had never seen his mistress. But having viewed her one day by accident, he became passionately in love with her. In despight of all danger he ventured to court her affection, by means of a female friend, whom he with much trouble got over to his interest. But both he and she lost all their labour, for they had to do with a truly virtuous woman. At length, despairing to prosper in his amours, he changed his love into hatred,

hatred, and meditated a moſt bloody revenge. To this effect he cunningly went and bought two parrots; one of which he taught to pronounce theſe words, *I ſaw my miſtreſs in bed with the falconer*; and the other, *For my part, I ſay nothing.* In a little time after theſe birds had learned their leſſon, the merchant having invited his friends to a great feaſt, when every body was ſeated at the table, theſe parrots began to repeat their leſſon. Now the falconer had taught theſe parrots to ſpeak theſe words in his own country language, which was different from that of the place, becauſe the maſter, miſtreſs, nor any of the ſervants, underſtood what they meant, nobody minded their repeating them. But this was not the caſe now; for, ſome of the gueſts, who happened to be the falconer's countrymen, no ſooner heard the parrots, but they forbore eating, and ſtared with the utmoſt amazement one at another. The merchant, aſtoniſhed at this, aſked them the reaſon. Do ye not underſtand, anſwered the gueſts, what theſe birds ſay? No replied the merchant. Why, they ſay, ſaid the gueſt that ſpoke firſt, that your falconer has made you a cuckold. The merchant was aſtoniſhed and confounded at theſe words, and begged pardon of his friends for having invited them to a place where ſo much uncleanneſs had been committed. The falconer alſo, the more to exaſperate his maſter againſt his wife, confeſſed the fact, and ſaid that it was true. Which put the huſband into ſo great a rage, that he ordered his wife to be put to death.

When they, that were ordered to execute her huſband's command, came to her, and with great ſorrow

sorrow acquainted her with their business, she told them that she was ready to suffer any punishment which her husband, who was her lord and sovereign master, thought fit to inflict upon her; but, that as she was innocent of the crime she was accused of, she could have wished he would, for the sake of his own future peace, have heard her first; for that, if her innocence should afterwards come to be known, his repentance would be then too late. This being reported to her husband, he sent for her into a little closet, whither he ordered her to come veiled, and bid her justify herself if she could. The parrots, said he, are no rational creatures, and therefore cannot be accused either of imposture or bribery: how then will you justify yourself against what they accuse you of?

You are bound, my dear lord, in duty and honour, answered the wife, to be well assured of the truth, in a case of this kind, before you condemn me to death; and there is an easy way by which you may know it: ask those gentlemen whether they observe any variety of relation in these parrots speech, or whether they only repeat the same set of words over and over again. . If they only repeat the same words, be assured they speak not of knowledge or design, and have only been taught to repeat them, and that it is a device made use of by your servant to provoke your undeserved anger against me, because he could not obtain those favours from me which he desired, and which he has long solicited, though I have been so charitable to his youth as not to accuse him to you of it. If it be thus, let the weight of your anger fall on him: if otherwise,

let

let me perish. The merchant judging, by her prudent advice, that she might not be guilty, went to his guests, carried them the parrots, and desired them to stay with him, and diligently observe, for two or three days, whether the birds spoke any thing else besides what they had heard. Which the guests accordingly did. The result of this was, that they found the parrots always in the same lesson, of which they faithfully informed the merchant, who then acknowledged the innocence of his wife, and was sensible of the malice of his servant. The falconer was now sent for, and instantly appeared with his hawk upon his fist. To whom the wife: Villain, said she, how didst thou dare to accuse me of so foul a crime? Because you were guilty, answered the servant. But he had no sooner uttered the words, when the hawk upon his fist flew in his face and tore out his eyes; and the husband acknowledged the injustice he was like to have been guilty of, and on his knees implored his wife's pardon.

This example, said Damna, pursuing his discourse, instructs us how heinous a thing it is to bear false witness; and that it always turns to our shame and confusion. Happy therefore is your majesty, who have no subject in your whole dominions wicked enough to be guilty of it. After Damna had done speaking, the lion, looking upon his mother, asked her opinion. I find, answered she, that you have a kindness for this most cunning villain; but, believe me, he will, if you pardon him, cause nothing but faction and disorder in your court. I beseech you, re‑
plied

plied the lion, to tell me who has so strongly prepossessed you against Damna. It is but too true, replied the queen-mother, that he has committed the crime that is laid to his charge. I know him to be guilty, but I shall not now discover the person who intrusted me with this secret. However, I will go to him, and ask him whether he will be willing that I should bring him in for a witness: and, so saying, she went home immediately, and sent for the leopard.

When he was come: This villain whom you have accused to me, said she, will escape the hands of justice, unless you appear yourself against him. Go, therefore, continued she, at my request, and boldly declare what thou knowest concerning Damna. Fear no danger in so honest a cause, for no ill shall befal thee. Madam, answered the leopard, you know that I could wish to be excused from this, but you also know that I am ready to sacrifice my life to your majesty's commands; dispose of me, therefore, as you please; I am ready to go wherever you command. With that she carried the leopard to the king; to whom, Sir, said she, here is an undeniable witness which I have to produce against Damna. Then the lion, addressing himself to the leopard, asked him what proof he had of the delinquent's treason? Sir, answered the leopard, I was willing to conceal this truth, on purpose, for some time, to see what reasons the cunning traitor would bring to justify himself; but now it is time your majesty knew all. On this the leopard made a long recital of what had passed between Kalila and her husband: which deposition, being made in the hearing of several

beasts,

beasts, was soon divulged far and near, and presently afterwards confirmed by a second testimony, which was the bear's, of whom I made mention before. After this the delinquent was asked what he had now to say for himself; but he had not a word to answer. This at length determined the lion to sentence that Damna, as a traitor, should be shut up between four walls, and there starved to death.

These chapters, concluded Pilpay, may it please you majesty, are lessons to deceivers and sycophants, that they ought to reform their manners, and I think have sufficiently made it appear, that slanderers and railers generally come to an unfortunate end; besides that, while they live, they render themselves odious to all human society. He, that plants thorns, must never expect to gather roses.

CHAP.

## CHAP. IV.

*How we ought to make choice of* FRIENDS; *and what advantage may be reaped from their conversation.*

YOU have now told me, said the king, to my infinite satisfaction, the story of a knave, who, under the false appearances of friendship, occasioned the death of an innocent person. I desire you next to inform me what benefit may be made of honest men and real friends in civil life. Your majesty, answered the Bramin, is to know, that honest men esteem and value nothing so much in this world as a real friend. Such an one is as it were another self, to whom we impart our most secret thoughts, who partakes of our joy, and comforts us in our affliction: add to this, that his company is an everlasting pleasure to us. But nothing can, perhaps, give your majesty a clearer or nobler idea of the pleasures of a reciprocal friendship than the following fable.

FABLE

## FABLE I.

*The* RAVEN, *the* RAT, *and the* PIDGEONS.

NEarly adjoining to Odorna there was once a moſt delightful place, which was extremely full of wild-fowl, and was therefore much frequented by the ſportſmen and fowlers. A raven one day accidentally eſpied in this place, at the foot of a tree, on the top of which ſhe had built her neſt, a certain fowler with a net in his hand. The poor raven was afraid at firſt, imagining it was herſelf that the fowler aimed at; but her fears ceaſed when ſhe obſerved the motions of the perſon, who, after he had ſpread his net upon the ground, and ſcattered ſome corn about it to allure the birds, went and hid himſelf behind a hedge, where he was no ſooner laid down, but a flock of pidgeons threw themſelves upon the corn, without hearkening to their chieftain, who would fain have hindered them, telling them, that they were not ſo raſhly to abandon themſelves to their paſſions. The prudent leader, who was an old pidgeon, called Montivaga, perceiving them ſo obſtinate, had many times a deſire to ſeparate himſelf from them; but fate, that imperiouſly controuls all living creatures, conſtrained him to follow the fortune of the reſt, ſo that he alighted upon the ground with his companions. It was not long after this before they all ſaw themſelves under the net, and juſt ready to fall into the fowler's hands. Well, ſaid Montivaga on this, mournfully, to them, what think you now? will you

you believe me another time, if it be possible that you may get away from this destruction? I see, continued he, perceiving how they fluttered to get loose, that every one of you minds his own safety only, never regarding what becomes of his companions; and, let me tell you, that this is not only an ungrateful, but a foolish, way of acting; we ought to make it our business to help one another, and it may be so charitable an action may save us all; let us all together strive to break the net. On this they all obeyed Montivaga, and so well bestirred themselves, that they tore the net up from the ground, and carried it up with them into the air. The fowler, on this, vexed to lose so fair a prey, followed the pidgeons, in hopes that the weight of the net would tire them.

In the mean time the raven, observing all this, said to herself, this is a very pleasant adventure, I will see the issue of it; and accordingly she took wing and followed them. Montivaga observing that the fowler had resolved to pursue them, This man, said he to his companions, will never give over pursuing us, till he has lost sight of us; therefore, to prevent our destruction, let us bend our flight to some thick wood, or some ruined castle, to the end that, when we are protected by some forest or thick wall, despair may force him to retire. This expedient had the desired success; for, having secured themselves among the boughs of a thick forest, where the fowler lost sight of them, he returned home, full sorely afflicted with the loss of his game and his net to boot.

As for the raven, she followed them still, out of curiosity to know how they got out of the

net,

net, that she might make use of the same secret upon the like occasion.

The pidgeons, thus quit of the fowler, were overjoyed; however, they were still troubled with the intanglements of the net, which they could not get rid of: but Montivaga, who was fertile in inventions, soon found a way for that. We must address ourselves, said he, to some intimate friend, who, setting aside all treacherous and by-ends, will go faithfully to work for our deliverance. I know a rat, continued he, that lives not far hence, a faithful friend of mine, whose name is Zirac; he, I know, will gnaw the net, and set us at liberty. The pidgeons, who desired nothing more, all entreated to fly to this friend; and, soon after, they arrived at the rat's hole, who came forth upon the fluttering of their wings; and, astonished and surprized to see Montivaga so intangled in the net, O! my dear friend, said he, how came you into this condition? To whom Montivaga replied, I desire you, my most faithful friend, first of all to disengage my companions. But Zirac, more troubled to see his friend bound than for all the rest, would needs pay his respect to him first; but Montivaga cried out, I conjure you once more, by our sacred friendship, to set my companions at liberty before me; for that besides, being their chieftain, I ought to take care for them in the first place, I am afraid the pains thou wilt take to unbind me will slacken thy good offices to the rest; whereas, the friendship thou hast for me will excite thee to hasten their deliverance, that thou mayest be sooner in a condition to give me my freedom. The rat, admiring the solidity of these arguments, applauded

plauded Montivaga's generosity, and fell to loosening the strangers; which was soon done; then he performed the same kind office for his friend.

Montivaga, thus at liberty, together with his companions, took his leave of Zirac, returning him a thousand thanks for his kindness. And, when they were gone, the rat returned to his hole.

The raven, having observed all this, had a great desire to be acquainted with Zirac. To which end he went to his hole, and called him by his name. Zirac, frighted to hear a strange voice, asked who he was? To which the raven answered, It is a raven who has some business of importance to impart to thee. What business, replied the rat, can you or I have together? we are enemies. Then the raven told him, he desired to list himself in the number of a rat's acquaintance, whom he knew to be so sincere a friend. I beseech you, answered Zirac, find out some other creature, whose friendship agrees better with your disposition. You lose your time in endeavouring to persuade me to such an incompatible reconciliation. Never stand upon incompatibilities, said the raven, but do a generous action, by affording an innocent person your friendship and acquaintance, when he desires it at your hands. You may talk to me of generosity till your lungs ache, replied Zirac, I know your tricks too well: in a word, we are creatures of so different species, that we can never be either friend or acquaintance. The example which I remember of the partridge, that over-
haftily

haſtily granted her friendſhip to a falcon, is a ſufficient warning to make me wiſer.

---

## FABLE II.
### The PARTRIDGE and the FALCON.

A Partridge, ſaid Zirac, keeping cloſe in his hole, but very obligingly purſuing his diſcourſe, was promenading at the foot of a hill, and tuning her throat, in her coarſe way, ſo delightfully, that a falcon flying that way, and hearing her voice, came towards her, and very civilly was going to aſk her acquaintance. Nobody, ſaid he to himſelf, can live without a friend; and it is the ſaying of the wiſe, that they, who want friends, labour under perpetual ſickneſs. With theſe thoughts he would fain have accoſted the partridge; but ſhe, perceiving him, eſcaped into a hole, all over in a cold ſweat for fear. The falcon followed her, and preſenting himſelf at the foot of the hole, My dear partridge, ſaid he, I own that I never had any great kindneſs hitherto for you, becauſe I did not know your merit; but, ſince my good fortune has now made me acquainted with your merry note, be pleaſed to give me yours. Tyrant, anſwered the partridge, let me alone, and labour not in vain to reconcile fire and water. Moſt amiable partridge, replied the falcon,

con, banish these idle fears, and be convinced that I love you, and desire that we may enter into a familiarity together: had I any other design, I would not trouble myself to court you with such soft language out of your hole. Believe me, I have such good pounces, that I would have seized a dozen other partridges in the time that I have been courting your affection; I am sure you will have reasons enough to be glad of my friendship; first, because no other falcon shall do you any harm while you are under my protection; secondly, because that, being in my nest, you will be honoured by the world; and, lastly, I will procure you a male to keep you company, and give you all the delights of love and a young progeny. It is impossible for me to think you can have so much kindness to me, replied the partridge; but, indeed should this be true, I ought not to accept your proposal; for you being the prince of birds, and of the greatest strength, and I a poor weak partridge, whenever I shall do any thing that displeases you, you will not fail to tear me to pieces. No, no, said the falcon, set your heart at rest for that; the faults that friends commit are easily pardoned. Much other discourse of this kind passed between them, and many doubts were started and answered to satisfaction, so that at length the falcon testified such an extraordinary friendship for the partridge, that she could no longer refuse coming out of her hole. And no sooner was she come forth, but the falcon tenderly embraced her, and carried her to his nest, where, for two or three days, he made it his whole business to divert her. The partridge, overjoyed to see herself so caressed, gave her tongue more liberty than

she

she had done before, and talked much of the cruelty and savage temper of the birds of prey. This began to offend the falcon, though, for the present, he dissembled it. One day, however, he unfortunately fell ill, which hindered him from going abroad in search of prey, so that he grew hungry, and, wanting victuals, he soon became melancholy, morose, and churlish. His being out of humour quickly alarmed the partridge, who kept herself, very prudently, close in a corner with a very modest countenance. But the falcon, soon after, no longer able to endure the importunities of his stomach, resolved to pick a quarrel with the poor partridge. To which purpose, It is not fitting, said he, that you should lie lurking there in the shade, while all the world is exposed to the heat of the sun. The partridge, trembling every joint of her, replied, King of birds, it is now night, and all the world is in the shade as well as I, nor do I know what sun you mean. Insolent baggage, replied the falcon, then you will make me either a liar or mad: and, so saying, he fell upon her, and tore her to pieces.

Do not believe, pursued the rat, that, upon the faith of your promises, I will lay myself at your mercy. Recollect yourself, answered the raven, and consider that it is not worth my while to fool my stomach with such a diminutive body as thine, it is therefore with no such intent I am talking with thee, but I know thy friendship may be beneficial to me; scruple not therefore to grant me this favour. The sages of old, replied the rat, admonish us to take care of being deluded by the fair words of our enemies, as

was

was a certain unfortunate man, whose story, if you please, I will relate to you.

## FABLE III.
### The MAN and the ADDER.

A Man, mounted upon a camel, once rode into a thicket, and went to rest himself in that part of it, whence a caravan was just departed, and where the people having left a fire, some sparks of it, being driven by the wind, had set a bush, wherein lay an adder, all in a flame. The fire environed the adder in such a manner, that he knew not how to escape, and was just giving himself over to destruction, when he perceived the man already mentioned, and, with a thousand mournful conjurations, begged of him to save his life. The man, on this, being naturally compassionate, said to himself, It is true, these creatures are enemies to mankind; however, good actions are of great value, even of the very greatest when done to our enemies, and whoever sows the seed of good works shall reap the fruit of blessings. After he had made this reflection, he took a sack, and tying it to the end of his lance, reached it over the flame to the adder, who flung himself into it; and, when he was safe in, the traveller pulled back the bag, and gave the adder leave to come forth, telling him he might go about his business, but hoped he would have the gratitude to make him a promise, never to do any more harm to men, since a man had done him so great a piece of service. To this the ungrateful creature answered, You much mistake both yourself and me; think not that I intend to be gone so calmly; no, my design is first to leave thee a parting blessing, and throw my venom upon thee and thy camel. Monster of ingratitude, replied the traveller, desist a moment at least, and tell me whether it be lawful to recompense good with evil! No, replied the adder it certainly is not; but, in acting in that manner, I shall do no more than what yourselves do every day; that is to say, retaliate good deeds with wicked actions, and requite benefits with ingratitude. You cannot prove this slanderous and wicked aspersion, replied the traveller; nay, I will venture to say, that if you can shew me any one other creature in the world that is of your opinion, I will consent to whatever punishment you think fit to inflict on me for the faults of my fellow-creatures. I agree to this willingly, answered the adder; and at the same time spying a cow, Let us propound our question, said he, to this creature before us, and we will see what answer she will make. The man consented, and so both of them accosting the cow, the adder put the question to her, how a good turn was to be requited? By its contrary, replied the cow, if you mean according to the custom of men; and this I know by sad experience. I belong, said she, to a man, to whom I have long been several ways extremely beneficial: I have been used to bring him a calf every year, and to supply his house with milk, butter, and cheese; but now I am grown old, and no longer in a condition to serve him as formerly

merly I did, he has put me in this pasture to fat me, with a design to sell me to a butcher, who is to cut my throat, and he and his friends are to eat my flesh: and is not this a requiting good with evil? On this the adder taking upon him to speak, said to the man, What say you now, are not your own customs a sufficient warrant for me to treat you as I intend to do? The traveller, not a little confounded at this ill-timed story, was cunning enough, however, to answer, this is a particular case only, and give me leave to say, one witness is not sufficient to convict me; therefore pray let me have another. With all my heart, replied the adder; let us address ourselves to this tree that stands here before us. The tree, having heard the subject of their dispute, gave his opinion in the following words: Among men, benefits are never requited but with ungrateful actions. I protect travellers from the heat of the sun, and yield them fruit to eat, and a delightful liquor to drink; nevertheless, forgetting the delight and benefit of my shade, they barbarously cut down my branches to make sticks and handles for hatchets, and saw my body to make planks and rafters. Is not this requiting good with evil? The adder, on this, looking upon the traveller, asked if he was satisfied? but he was in such a confusion, that he knew not what to answer. However, in hopes to free himself from the danger that threatened him, said to the adder, I desire only one favour more; let us be judged by the next beast we meet; give me but that satisfaction, it is all I crave; you know life is sweet; suffer me therefore to beg for the means of continuing it. While they were thus
parleyi

parleying together, a fox, paſſing by, was ſtopped by the adder, who conjured him to put an end to their controverſy. The fox, upon this, deſiring to know the ſubject of their diſpute; ſaid the traveller, I have done this adder a ſignal piece of ſervice, and he would fain perſuade me that, for my reward, he ought to do me a miſchief. If he means to act by you as you men do by others, he ſpeaks nothing but what is true, replied the fox; but, that I may be better able to judge between you, let me underſtand what ſervice it is that you have done him? The traveller was very glad of this opportunity of ſpeaking for himſelf, and recounted the whole affair to him; he told him after what manner he had reſcued him out of the flames with that little ſack which he ſhewed him. How! ſaid the fox, laughing out-right, would you pretend to make me believe that ſo large an adder as this could get into ſuch a little ſack? it is impoſſible. Both the man and the adder, on this, aſſured him of the truth of that part of the ſtory; but the fox poſitively refuſed to believe it. At length, ſaid he, words will never convince me of this monſtrous improbability; but if the adder will go into it again, to convince me of the truth of what you ſay, I ſhall then be able to judge of the reſt of this affair. That I will do moſt willingly, replied the adder; and at the ſame time put himſelf into the ſack. Then ſaid the fox to the traveller, now you are the maſter of your enemy's life; and, I believe, you need not be long in reſolving what treatment ſuch a monſter of ingratitude deſerves of you. With that the traveller tied up the mouth of the ſack, and, with a great ſtone, never left off beating

ing it till he had pounded the adder to death; and, by that means, put an end to his fears, and the dispute, at once.

This fable, pursued the rat, informs us that there is no trusting to the fair words of an enemy, for fear of falling into the like misfortunes. You say very true, replied the raven, in all this; but what I have to answer to it is, that we ought to understand how to distinguish friends from enemies; and, when you have learned that art, you will know I am no terrible or treacherous foe, but a sincere and hearty friend; for, I protest to thee, in the most solemn manner, that what I have seen thee do for thy friend the pidgeon, and his companions, has taken such root in me, that I cannot live without an acquaintance with thee; and I swear I will not depart from hence till thou hast granted me thy friendship. Zirac, perceiving at length that the raven really dealt frankly and cordially with him, replied, I am happy to find that you are sincere in all this; pardon my fears, and now hear me acknowledge, that I think it is an honour for me to wear the title of thy friend; and, if I have so long withstood thy importunities, it was only to try thee, and to shew thee that I want neither wit nor policy, that thou mayest know hereafter how far I may be able to serve thee. And, so saying, he came forward; but even now he did not venture fairly out, but stopped at the entrance of his hole. Why dost thou not come boldly forth? demanded the raven: is it because thou art not yet assured of my affection? That is not the reason, answered the rat, but I am afraid of thy companions upon the trees. Set thy heart

at

at reſt for that, replied the raven, they ſhall reſpect thee as their friend: for, it is a cuſtom among
us, that, when one of us enters into a league of
friendſhip with a creature of another ſpecies, we all
eſteem and love that creature. The rat, upon the
faith of theſe words, came out to the raven, who
careſſed him with extraordinary demonſtrations
of friendſhip; ſwearing to him an inviolable ami-
ty, and requeſting him to go and live with him,
near the habitation of a certain neighbouring tortoiſe, of whom he gave a very noble character.
Command me henceforward in all things, replied
Zirac; for, I have ſo great an inclination for you,
that from henceforward I will for ever follow
you as your ſhadow; and, to tell you the truth,
this is not the proper place of my reſidence; I
was only compelled, ſome time ſince, to take
ſanctuary in this hole by reaſon of an accident,
of which I would give you the relation, if I thought
it might not be offenſive to you. My dear friend,
replied the raven, can you have any ſuch fears?
or rather are you not convinced that I ſhare in all
your concerns? But the tortoiſe, added he, whoſe
friendſhip is a very conſiderable acquiſition, which
you cannot fail of, will be no leſs glad to hear the
recital of your adventures: come, therefore,
away with me to her, continued he; and, at the
ſame time, he took the rat in his bill, and carried him to the tortoiſe's dwelling, to whom he
related what he had ſeen Zirac do. She congratulated the raven for having acquired ſo perfect a
friend, and careſſed the rat at a very high rate;
who, for his part, was too much a courtier not
to teſtify how ſenſible he was of all her civilities.
After many compliments on all ſides, they went
all

all three to walk by the banks of a purling rivulet; and, having made choice of a place somewhat distant from the highway, the raven desired Zirac there to relate his adventures, which he did in the following manner.

## FABLE IV.

### The Adventures of ZIRAC.

I Was born, said Zirac, and lived many years, in a city of India called Marout, where I made choice of a place to reside in, that seemed to be the habitation of silence itself, that I might live without disturbance. Here I enjoyed long the greatest earthly felicity, and tasted the sweets of a quiet life, in company with some other rats, honest creatures, of my own humour. There was also in our neighbourhood, I must inform you, a certain dervise, who every day remained idly in his habitation while his companion went to begging. He constantly, however, ate a part of what the other brought home, and kept the remainder for his supper. But, when he sate down to his second meal, he never found his dish in the same condition that he left it. For, while he was in his garden, I always filled my belly, and constantly called my companions to partake with me, who were no less mindful of their duty to nature than myself. The dervise, on this, constantly finding his pittance diminished, flew out at length into a great rage, and looked into his books for some receipt, or some engine, to apprehend us; but all that nothing availed him, I was still more cunning

than

than he. One unfortunate day, however, one of his friends, who had been a long journey, entered into his cell to vifit him; and, after they had dined, they fell into a difcourfe concerning travel. The dervife, our good purveyor, among other things, afked his friend what he had feen, that was moft rare and curious, in his travels. To whom the traveller began to recount what he had obferved moft worthy remark; but, as he was ftudying to give him a defcription of the moft delightful places through which he had paffed, the dervife ftill interrupted him, from time to time, with the noife which he made, by clapping his hands one againft the other, and ftamping with his foot againft the ground, to fright us away: for, indeed, we made frequent fallies upon his provifion, never regarding his prefence nor his company. At length, the traveller taking it in dudgeon that the dervife gave fo little ear to him, told him, in down-right terms, that he did ill to detain him there, to trouble him with telling ftories he did not attend to, and make a fool of him. Heaven forbid! replied the dervife, altogether furprifed, that I fhould make a fool of a perfon of your merit: I beg your pardon for interrupting you, but there is in this place a neft of rats that will eat me up to the very ears before they have done; and there is one above the reft fo bold, that he even has the impudence to come and bite me by the toes as I lie afleep, and I know not how to catch the felonious devil. The traveller, on this, was fatisfied with the dervife's excufes; and replied, certainly there is fome myftery in this: this accident brings to my mind a remarkable ftory, which I will relate to you, provided you will hearken to me with a little better attention.

## FABLE V.
### A Husband and his Wife.

ONE day, continued the traveller, as I was on my journey, the bad weather constrained me to stop at a town where I had several acquaintances of different ranks; and, being unable to proceed on my journey for the continuance of the rain, I went to lodge at one of my friends, who received me very civilly. After supper, he put me to bed in a chamber that was parted from his own by a very thin wainscot only, so that, in despight of my ears, I heard all his private conversation with his wife. To morrow, said he, I intend to invite the principal burghers of the town, to divert my friend, who has done me the honour to come and see me. You have not sufficient wherewithal to support your family, answered his wife, and yet you talk of being at great expences: rather think of sparing that little you have for the good of your children, and let feasting alone. This is a man of great religion and piety, replied the husband, and I ought to testify my joy on seeing him, and to give my other friends an opportunity of hearing his pious conversation; nor be you in care for the small expence that will attend this. The providence of God is very great, and we ought not to take too much care for to-morrow, lest what befel the wolf befal us.

# FABLE VI.

## The HUNTER and the WOLF.

ONE day, continued the husband, a great hunter returning from the chace of a deer, which he had killed, unexpectedly espied a wild boar coming out of a wood, and making directly towards him. Very good, cried the hunter, this beast comes very good-naturedly, he will not a little augment my provision. With that he bent his bow, and let fly his arrows with so good an aim, that he wounded the boar to death. Such, however, are the unforeseen events that attend too covetous a care for the necessaries of life, that this fair beginning was but a prelude to a very fatal catastrophe. For, the beast, feeling himself wounded, ran with so much fury at the hunter, that he ript up his belly with his tusks in such a manner, that they both fell dead upon the place.

At the very moment when this happened, there passed by a wolf half famished, who, seeing so much victuals lying upon the ground, was in an extacy of joy. However, said he to himself, I must not be prodigal of all this good food; but it behoves me to husband my good fortune, to make my provision hold out the longer. Being very hungry, however, he very prudently resolved to fill his belly first, and make his store for the future afterwards. Not willing, however, to waste any part of his treasure, he was for eating his meat, and, if possible, having it too; he therefore resolved to fill his belly with what was least delicate; and accordingly began with the string of the bow, which was made of gut; but he had no sooner snapt the string, but the bow, which was highly bent, gave him such a terrible thump upon the breast, that he fell stone dead upon the other bodies.

This fable, said the husband, pursuing his discourse, instructs us that we ought not to be too greedily covetous. Nay, said the wife, if this be the effect of saving, e'en invite whom you please to-morrow.

The company was accordingly invited; but, the next day, as the wife was getting dinner ready, and making a sort of sauce with honey, she saw a rat fall into the honey-pot, which turned her stomach, and stopped the making of that part of the entertainment. Unwilling, therefore, to make use of the honey, she carried it to the market, and, when she parted with it, took pitch in exchange. I was then, by accident, by her, and asked her why she made such a disanvantageous exchange for her honey? because, said she in my ear, it is not worth so much to me as the pitch. Then I presently perceived there was some mystery in the affair, which was beyond my comprehension. It is the same with this rat: he would never be so bold, had he not some reason for it which we are ignorant of. The rats, continued he, in this part of the world, are a cunning, covetous, and proud, generation; they heap money as much as the misers of our own species; and, when one of them is possessed of a considerable sum, he becomes a prince among them, and has his set of comrades, who would die to serve him,

as

as they live by him; for, he disburses money for their purchases of food, &c. of one another, and they live his slaves in perfect idleness. And, for my part, I am apt to believe that this is the case with this impudent rat; that he has a number of slaves of his own species at command, to defend and uphold him in his audacious tricks, and that there is money hidden in his hole.

The dervise no sooner heard the traveller talk of money, but he took a hatchet, and so bestirred himself, that, having cleft the wall, he soon discovered my treasure, to the value of a thousand deniers of gold, which I had heaped together with great labour and toil. These had long been my whole pleasure; I told them every day; I took delight to handle them, and tumble upon them, placing all my happiness in that exercise. But to return to the story. When the gold tumbled out, Very good, said the traveller, had I not reason to attribute the insolence of these rats to some unknown cause.

I leave you to judge in what a desperate condition I was, when I saw my habitation ransacked after this manner. I resolved on this to change my lodging; but all my companions left me; so that I had a thorough experience of the truth of the proverb, *no money, no friend*. Friends, now-a-days, love us no longer than our friendship turns to their advantage. I have heard, among the men, that one day a wealthy and a witty man was asked, how many friends he had: As for friends a-la-mode, said he, I have as many as I have crowns; but as for real friends, I must stay till I come to be in want, and then I shall know.

While I was pondering, however, upon the accident that had befallen me, I saw a rat pass along, who had been heretofore used to profess himself so much devoted to my service, that you would have thought he could not have lived a moment out of my company. I called to him, and asked him, why he shunned me like the rest? Thinkest thou, said the ungrateful and impudent villain, that we are such fools to serve thee for nothing? when thou wert rich, we were thy servants; but, now thou art poor, believe me, we will not be the companions of thy poverty. Alas! thou oughtest not to despise the poor, said I, because they are the beloved of providence. It is very true, answered he; but not such poor as thou art; for, providence takes care of those among men, who have, for the sake of religion, forsaken the world; not those whom the world has forsaken. Miserably angry was I with myself for my former generosities to such a wretch; but I could not tell what to answer to such a cutting expression. I staid, however, notwithstanding my misfortunes, with the dervise, to see how he would dispose of the money he had taken from me, and I observed that he gave one half to his friend, and that each of them laid their shares under their pillows. On seeing this, an immediate thought came into my mind to go and regain this money. To this purpose I stole softly to the dervise's bedside, and was just going to carry back my treasure; but, unfortunately, his friend, who, unperceived by me, observed all my actions, threw his bed staff at me with so good a will, that he had almost broke my foot, which obliged me to recover my hole with all the peed I could, though not without
some

some difficulty. About an hour after, I crept out again, believing by this time the traveller might be asleep also. But he was too diligent a centinel, and too much afraid of losing his good fortune. However, I plucked up a good heart, went forward, and was already got to the dervise's bed's-head, when my rashness had like to have cost me my life. For, the traveller gave me a second blow upon the head, that stunned me in such a manner, that I could hardly find my hole again. At the same instant he also threw his bed-staff at me a third time; but, missing me, I recovered my sanctuary, where I was no sooner set down in safety, but I protested never more to pursue the recovery of a thing which had cost me so much pains and jeopardy. In pursuance of this resolution, I left the dervise's habitation, and retired to that place where you saw me with the pidgeon. The tortoise was extremely well pleased with the recital of the rat's adventures, and, at the same time embracing him, You have done well, said she, to quit the world, and the intrigues of it, since they afford us no perfect satisfaction. All those who are turmoiled with avarice and ambition do but labour their own ruin like a certain cat, which I once knew, whose adventure you will not be displeased to hear.

16            FABLE

## FABLE VII.

### *The* RAVENOUS CAT.

A Certain perſon, whom I have often ſeen, continued the tortoiſe, bred up a cat very frugally in his own houſe: he gave her enough to ſuffice nature, though nothing ſuperfluous; and ſhe might, if ſhe pleaſed, have lived very happily with him; but ſhe was very ravenous, and, not content with her ordinary food, hunted about in every corner for more. One day, paſſing by a dove-houſe, ſhe ſaw ſome young pidgeons, that were hardly fledged, and preſently her teeth watered for a taſte of thoſe delicate viands. With this reſolution, up ſhe boldly mounted into the dove-houſe, never minding whether the maſter were there or not, and was preſently, with great joy, preparing to ſatisfy her voluptuous deſires. But the maſter of the place no ſooner ſaw this epicure of a cat enter, but he ſhut up the doors, and ſtopped all the holes at which it was poſſible for her to get out again, and ſo beſtirred himſelf, that he caught the felonious baggage, and hanged her up at the corner of the pidgeon-houſe. Soon after this, the owner of the cat paſſing that way, and ſeeing his cat hanged, Unfortunate greedygut, ſaid he, hadſt thou been contented with thy meaner food, thou hadſt not been now in this condition! Thus, continued he, moralizing on the ſpectacle, inſatiable gluttons are the procurers of their own untimely ends. Alas! the felicities of this world are uncertain, and of no continuance. Wiſe men, I well remember, ſay

there

there is no reliance upon these six things, nor any thing of fidelity to be expected from them.

1. From a cloud; for, it disperses in an instant.

2. From feigned friendship; for, it passes away like a flash of lightening.

3. From a woman's love; for, it changes upon every frivolous fancy.

4. From beauty; for, the least injury of time, misfortune, or a disease, destroys it.

5. From false prayers; for, they are but smoke.

6. And from the enjoyments of the world; for, they all vanish in a moment.

Men of judgement, replied the rat, are all of this opinion; they never labour after these vain things; there is nothing but the acquisition of a real friend can tempt us to the expectation of a lasting happiness. The raven then spoke in his turn. There is no earthly pleasure or advantage, said he, like a true friend; which I shall endeavour to prove by the recital of the following story.

## FABLE VIII.

### The TWO FRIENDS.

A Certain person, of a truly noble and generous disposition, once heard, as he lay in bed, some body knocking at his door at an unseasonable hour. Something surprised at it, he, without stirring out of his place, first asked, Who

was

was there? But, when by the answer he understood that it was one of his best friends, he immediately arose, put on his clothes, and, ordering his servant to light a candle, went and opened the door. So soon as he he saw him, dear friend, said he, I at all times rejoice to see you, but doubly now, because I promise myself, from this extraordinary visit, that I can be of some service to you. I cannot imagine your coming so late to be for any other reason, but either to borrow money, to desire me to be your second, or because you want female company to divert some sudden melancholy: and I am very happy in that I can assure you that I am provided to serve you in any of these requests. If you want money, my purse is full, and it is open to all your occasions. If you are to meet with your enemy, my arm and sword are at your service. Or, if any amorous desire bring you abroad, here is my maid, handsome enough, and ready to give you a civil entertainment. In a word, whatever lies in my power is at your service. There is nothing I have less occasion for, answered his friend, than all these things which you proffer me. I only came to understand the condition of your health, fearing the truth of an unlucky and disastrous dream.

While the raven was reciting this fable, our set of friends beheld at a distance a little wild goat making towards them with an incredible swiftness.

They all took it for granted, by her speed, that she was pursued by some hunter, and they immediately without ceremony separated every one to take care of himself. The tortoise slipt
into

into the water, the rat crept into a hole which he accidentally found there, and the raven hid himself among the boughs of a very high tree. In the mean time the goat stopt all on a sudden, and stood to rest itself by the side of the fountain; when the raven, who looked about every way, perceiving nobody, called to the tortoise, who immediately peeped above the water; and, seeing the goat afraid to drink, Drink boldly, said the tortoise, for, the water is very clear. Which the goat having done, Pray tell me, cried the tortoise, what is the reason you seem to be in such a fright? Reason enough, replied the goat; for, I have just made my escape from the hands of a hunter who pursued me with an eager chace. Come, said the tortoise, I am glad you are safe, and I have an offer to make you, if you can like our company, stay here, and be one of our friends; you will find, I assure you, our hearts honest and our conversation beneficial. Wise men, continued she, say, that the number of friends lessens trouble; and that, if a man had a thousand friends, he ought to reckon them no more than as one; but, on the other side, if a man has but one enemy, he ought to reckon that one for a thousand, so dangerous and so desperate a thing is an avowed enemy. After this discourse, the raven and the rat entered into company with the goat, and shewed her a thousand civilities, with which she was so taken, that she promised to stay there as long as she lived.

These four friends, after this, lived in perfect good harmony a long while, and spent their time very pleasantly together. But, one day, as the tortoise, the rat, and the raven, were met, as

they

they used to do, by the side of the fountain, the goat was missing; this very much troubled the other friends, as they knew not what accident might have befallen her. They soon came to a resolution, however, to seek for and assist her; and presently the raven mounted up into the air, to see what discoveries he could make; and, looking round about him, at length, to his great sorrow, saw at a distance the poor goat entangled in a hunter's net. He immediately dropt down on this, to acquaint the rat and tortoise with what he had seen; and you may be well assured these ill tidings extremely afflicted all the three friends. We have professed a strict friendship together, and lived long happily in it, said the tortoise, and it will be shameful now to break through it, and leave our innocent and good-natured friend to destruction; no, we must find some way, continued she, to deliver the poor goat out of captivity. On this, said the raven to the rat, remember now, O excellent Zirac! thy own talents, and exert them for the public good; there is none but you can set our friend at liberty; and the business must be quickly done, for fear the huntsman lay his clutches upon her. Doubt not but I will gladly do my endeavour, replied the rat; therefore let us go immediately, left we lose time. The raven on this took up Zirac in his bill, and carried him to the place; where, being arrived, he fell without delay to gnawing the meshes that held the goat's foot, and had almost set him at liberty by that time the tortoise arrived. So soon as the goat perceived this slow-moving friend, she sent forth a loud cry: Oh! said she, why have you ventured yourself

self to come hither? Alas! replied the tortoise, I could no longer endure your absence. Dear friend, said the goat, your coming to this place troubles me more than the loss of my own liberty: for, if the hunter should happen to come at this instant, what will you do to make your escape? for my part I am almost unbound, and my swift heels will preserve me from falling into his hands; the raven will find safety in his wings; the rat will run into any hole; only you, that is so slow of foot, will become the hunter's prey.

No sooner had the goat spoken the words but the hunter appeared; and the goat, being loosed, ran away; the raven mounted into the sky, the rat slipped into a hole, and, as the goat had said, only the slow-paced tortoise remained without help.

When the hunter arrived, he was not a little surprised to see his net broken. This was no small vexation to him, and made him look narrowly about, to see if he could discover who had done him the injury; and unfortunately, in searching, he spied the tortoise. Oh! said he, very well, I am very glad to see you here; I find I shall not go home empty-handed, however, at last: here is a plump tortoise, and that is worth something, I'm sure. With that he took the tortoise up, put it in his sack, threw the sack over his shoulder, and so was trudging home.

When he was gone, the three friends came from their several places, and met together, when, missing the tortoise, they easily judged what was become of her. Then, sending forth a thousand sighs, they made most doleful lamentations, and

shed

shed a torrent of tears. At length the raven interrupting this sad harmony, Dear friends, said he, our moans and sorrows do the tortoise no good; we ought, instead of this, if it be possible, to think of a way to save her life. The sages of former ages have informed us, that there are four sorts of persons that are never known but upon the proper occasions; men of courage in fight; men of honesty in business; a wife in her husband's misfortunes; and a true friend in extreme necessity. We find, alas! our dear friend the tortoise is in a sad condition, and therefore we must, if possible, succour her. It is well advised, replied the rat, and now I think on it, an expedient is come into my head. Let the goat go and shew herself in the hunter's eye, who will then be sure to lay down his sack to run after her. Very well advised, replied the goat, I will pretend to be lame, and run limping at a little distance before him, which will encourage him to follow me, and so draw him a good way from his sack, which will give the rat time to set our friend at liberty. This stratagem had so good a face, that it was soon approved by them all, and immediately the goat ran halting before the hunter, and seemed to be so feeble and faint, that the hunter thought he had her safe in his clutches; and so, laying down his sack, ran after the goat with all his might. That cunning creature suffered him ever and anon almost to come up to her, and then led him another wild-goose chace, till in short, she had fairly dragged him out of sight; which the rat perceiving, he came and gnawed the string that tied

the

the fack, and let out the tortoife, who went and hid herfelf in a thick bufh.

At length the hunter tired with running in vain after his prey, left off the chace and returned to his fack: Here, faid he, I have fomething fafe however; thou art not quite fo fwift of foot as this plaguy goat; and, if thou wert, art too faft here to find the way to make thy legs of any ufe to thee: fo faying he went to the bag; but there miffing the tortoife he was in amaze, and thought himfelf in a region of hobgoblins and fpirits. He could not but ftand and blefs himfelf, that a goat fhould free herfelf out of his nets, and by and by run hopping before him, and make a fool of him; and that in the mean while a tortoife, a poor feeble creature, fhould break the ftring of a fack, and make its efcape. All thefe confiderations ftruck him with fuch a panic that he ran home as if a thoufand robingood-fellows or raw-head and bloody-bones had been at his heels. After which the four friends met together again, congratulated each other on their efcapes, and made new proteftations of friendfhip, and fwore never to feparate till death parted them.

CHAP.

## CHAP. V.

*That we ought always to distrust our* ENEMIES, *and be, if possible, perfectly informed of whatever passes among them.*

WE are now, said Dabschelim, most excellent man! come to the fifth chapter; which is to prove, that no person of judgement and discretion ought to hope for friendship from his enemies. Teach me therefore, most venerable sage, since I must never expect good offices from them, which way to avoid their treasons. We ought, replied the bramin, always to distrust our enemies; when they make a show of friendship, it is only to cover their evil designs. Whoever confides in an enemy, believe me, will be deceived, like the owl in the fable which I am going to recite to your majesty.

FABLE

# FABLE I.

## The RAVENS and the OWLS.

IN the north-weſt parts of Zamardot*, continued Pilpay, there is a mountain whoſe top reaches above the clouds; and near the top of this mountain there once ſtood a tree whoſe boughs ſeemed to reach heaven; and theſe boughs were all laden with the neſts of a vaſt number of ravens, who were all the ſubjects of a king called Birouz. One night the king of the owls, who was called *Chabahang*, that is to ſay, *fly by night*, came at the head of his army (for, the birds of that nation are all under the government of their particular monarchs) to plunder the ravens neſts, againſt whom he had an ancient hatred. That night however they could do no more than make preparations for their intended enterprize, and by the vile noiſe of their ſcreams defy the enemy. The next day Birouz called a council, to deliberate what means they ſhould make uſe of to defend themſelves from the aſſaults of the owls. On which five of the ableſt politicians of his court, underſtanding his majeſty's intentions, gave their advice one after another in the following words. Great monarch, ſaid the firſt, we can think of nothing but what your majeſty has unqueſtionably already thought of before us. Nevertheleſs, ſince it is your pleaſure that we ſhould ſpeak in order what we judge moſt expedient

---

* Zamardot is accounted the moſt mountainous country of all the eaſt.

to revenge ourselves upon the owls, I shall only presume to observe to your majesty, that our best politicians have always held for a maxim, that no prince ought ever to attack an enemy stronger than himself: to do otherwise, is to build upon the current of a swift river. Sir, said the second, all I have to say, is, that flight becomes none but mean and cowardly souls: it is more noble to take arms and revenge the affront we have received than tamely to bear it, were we sure it would be no worse. A prince can never be at rest, if he does not carry terror into the country and into the soul of his enemy. When he had done speaking, the third, coming to give his opinion, said, I do not blame the counsel of my brethren who have already spoken; nor do I think either, or what may be deduced from both, sufficient: if I may presume to speak freely, my advice is, that your majesty send spies to discover the strength and condition of the enemy; and, according to the tenor of their reports, let us make war or peace: it is the duty of a king to preserve peace in his own kingdom, if it may be done without great disadvantages, as well for the repose of his own mind as for the ease of his subjects. War, we all know, is never to be declared but against those that disturb the public tranquillity; and, even in regard to such, if the enemy be too powerful, we must have recourse to artifice and stratagem, and make use of all opportunities that present themselves to vanquish him by cunning and policy. When this politician had thus given in his opinion, the fourth took his turn, and laid before the king, That, in his opinion, it was better for a prince even to

quit

quit his country than to expose a people to lose the reputation of their arms, who had always been victorious over their enemies. That even though it should be found that the enemies were the stronger, it would yet be a shame for the ravens to submit themselves to the owls, who had all along been under their subjection. And finally, that it was requisite to penetrate their designs, and resolve rather to fight than undergo an ignominious yoke, since loss of life was less to be dreaded than loss of reputation.

The king, after he had heard these four ministers, made a signal to the fifth to speak in his turn. This vizer, or minister, was called *Carchenas*, or the *Intelligent*. And the king, who had a particular confidence in him, desired him to tell him sincerely what he thought was best to be done in this affair. What say you, Carchenas? said the monarch, what shall we do? shall we declare war, or propound peace, or abandon our country? Sir, replied Carchenas, since you order me to speak with freedom, my opinion is, that we ought not to attack the owls, for this plain reason, that they are more numerous than we. We must make use of prudence, a virtue that has frequently a greater share in successes than either strength or riches. But, before your majesty take your final resolution, let me advise, that you consult your ministers once more, and give them an opportunity of declaring their opinions a second time; now that they are each of them acquainted with what is to be said on the other side, their councils may assist you to bring about your designs with success. Great rivers are always swelled by many rivulets. For my part,

part, I neither love war, nor am for base and dastardly submission. It is not for men of honour to desire that they may have long life, but that they may leave to posterity examples of virtue worthy of admiration: nor ought we meanly to take care of our lives at the expence of our country's safety, but to expose them upon all occasions where honour calls us, considering it is better never to have been than to live ignobly. Permit me to add, that my final advice is, that your majesty shew not the least fear in this conjuncture; and that you take your resolutions in private that your enemies may not penetrate into your designs.

Here one of the other ministers, interrupting Carchenas, said, with some earnestness, How! what mean you by this advice, so different from the tenor of the beginning of your speech? Wherefore are councils held but to debate among several? and wherefore would you have an affair of this consequence decided in a private manner? Affairs of princes, replied Carchenas, are not like those of merchants, which are to be communicated to the whole society: and there is a difference between hearing the advice of others and communicating our designs to them. The secrets of kings cannot be discovered but by their counsellors or ambassadors. And who knows but there may be spies in this very place who hear us, with an intent to disclose our resolutions to our enemies, who upon their report will prevent our enterprizes, or at least disorder our determinations? Wise men say, that if you will have a secret, take care to keep it a secret from all the world, not only from enemies but from friends.

friends. And let me tell you, sir, that monarch, who does not observe this rule, will run the hazard of being betrayed, as was the king of Quechemir. Upon this Birouz, who was very curious, commanded Carchenas to tell him the history.

## FABLE II.

### The KING and his MISTRESS.

IN the city of Quechemir there once reigned a king no less just than powerful, who had a mistress so surpassingly beautiful, that all persons that beheld her were in love with her. The king himself doated on her to that degree, that he would never be out of her company: but such was the misfortune of their destiny, that she was far from loving the king so dearly as she was beloved by him. The affection of the king, in short, flattered her vanity, but never touched her heart; which being always made, however, to harbour some particular amour or other, she once suffered herself to be possessed with a violent passion for a page, who was handsome and well proportioned, even to admiration. She soon informed him by her glances what sentiments she had for him, and the ogling youth as soon instructed her that she could not apply herself to a young spark that was more inclined to make his advantage of so fair a fortune. In short, there wanted nothing but an opportunity to get together in private.

In the midst of this expectation of happiness, it happened, however, that one day, as the king was sitting with his mistress, and gazing on her with delight, the page, who was standing in the same chamber, cast his eyes from time to time upon the charming lady; while she, on the other hand, fixed hers upon the page, with an air so passionate, that the king plainly perceived it. He understood but too well that silent language, and was so enraged with jealousy and distraction, that he immediately resolved to put them both to death. However, dissembling his design, because he would not act with too much precipitation, he re-entered his apartment, where he spent the night in miserable uneasiness and disquiet. The next morning, as soon as he arose, he heard the complaints of his subjects, as was his usual custom; and, after he had given satisfaction to his people, entered into his cabinet in great disorder of mind, and thither sent for his chief minister, and discovered to him his design to poison both his mistress and the page. The vizir, having heard his reasons, told him, that he could not but approve them, and promised to keep the secret. From his master's closet he immediately went home; where finding his daughter extremely pensive, he asked the reason. Father, said she, the king's favourite mistress has publicly affronted me; I am distracted at it; and, if I do not revenge myself, it is not for want of good will. Comfort yourself, replied the minister, take my word for it you will soon be delivered from your pain.

Now, as the women are naturally very curious, the daughter, from this hint, continually pressed her father to know after what manner she should

be

be revenged on her enemy; and he was at length so weak as to reveal to her the king's defign. It is true, fhe fwore not to difcover it. But, an hour or two after, the king's miſtrefs's eunuch coming to vifit the minifter's daughter, with an intention to comfort her, and extenuate the affront fhe had received; and, to that purpofe, telling her, that we ought to bear with our neighbour's faults: Ay, ay, faid the lady, interrupting him, with a difdainful fmile, let her alone, fhe has not long to play her proud pranks. Upon which the eunuch preſſed her fo earneſtly to explain her meaning, that fhe could hold no longer, but told him every word that her father had faid to her, after fhe had made him alfo fwear that he would inviolably keep the fecret. The eunuch, however, did not think an oath of that kind very binding; and, in fhort, he no fooner left her, but believing himfelf much more obliged to break than to keep his proteftations of fecrecy, he went to the king's miſtrefs, and revealed to her the violent refolution which the king had taken. There needed no more than the knowledge of the intent of the king, you may be fure, to incenfe the lady to try all ways to prevent and to be revenged on him. In ſhort, fhe fent away privately for the page, with whom fhe took fuch meafures, that the king was found next morning dead in his bed.

You fee by this ftory, continued Carchenas, that princes are not to difcover their fecrets to any, at leaft not to any but thofe of whofe difcretion and fidelity they have had conftant and affured proofs. But of what nature are the fecrets,

crets, said Birouz, which it most of all concerns us to conceal? Sir, answered Carchenas, there are many kinds of secrets; some are of such a nature, that princes are not to entrust any body but themselves with them; that is to say, they ought to keep them so concealed that nobody may be able, from any thing they see, even to make the least guess at them: and others there are, which though they ought to be kept most sacredly from the general knowledge, yet they may be communicated to faithful ministers for their advice and council.

Birouz finding that Carchenas spoke nothing but reason, withdrew from the rest of the council, and shut himself up with him in his cabinet; and, before he discoursed at large concerning the business in question, he desired him to tell him the fatal original of the deadly and hereditary hatred betwen the ravens and the owls. Sir, answered Carchenas, a few words alone produced that cruel animosity, the terrible effects of which you have so oft experienced. The story at large is this.

## FABLE III.

*The original of the hatred between the Ravens and the Owls.*

IT once happened that, in the neighbourhood of this our delightful habitation, a flight of birds assembled to choose themselves a king; and every different species among them put in his pretentions to the crown. At length, however, there were

*several*

several that gave their voices for the owl, because Minerva, the goddess of wisdom, had made choice of the owl for her peculiar bird: but a vast number of others being strenuous in their resolution never to obey so deformed a creature, the diet broke up, and they fell one upon another with so much fury, that several on all sides were slain. The fight, however, probably would have lasted longer than it did, had not a certain bird, in order to part them, bethought himself of crying out to the combatants, No more civil wars! Why do you spill one another's blood in vain? here is a raven coming, let us all agree to make him our judge and arbitrator; he is a person of judgement, and whose years have gained him experience. The birds unanimously consented to this; and when the raven arrived, and had informed himself of the occasion of the quarrel, he thus delivered himself: Are you such fools and madmen, gentlemen, says he, to choose for your king a bird, that draws after him nothing but misfortune? Will you set up a fly instead of a griffin? Why do you not rather make choice of a falcon, who is eminent for his courage and agility? or else a peacock, who treads with a majestic gait, and carries a train of starry eyes on his tail? why do you not rather raise an eagle to the throne, who is the emblem of royalty? or, lastly, a griffin, who, only by the motion and noise of his wings makes the mountains tremble? But, though there were no such birds as these that I have named in the world, surely it were better for you to live without a king than subject yourselves to such a horrid creature as an owl! for, though he has the physiognomy of a cat, he has no wit; and what is yet more insupportable, notwithstanding that he is so abominably ugly, he is as proud as a fine lady at a public feast; and what ought, if possible, to render him yet more despicable in our eyes, he hates the light of that magnificent body that enlivens all nature. Therefore, gentlemen, lay aside a design so prejudicial to your honour, proceed to the election of another king, and do nothing that you may be sure to repent of afterwards. Choose a king that may comfort you in your distresses, and remember the story of the rabbit, who, calling himself the moon's ambassador, expelled the elephants out of his country.

## FABLE IV.

### *The* ELEPHANTS *and the* RABBITS.

THERE happened once, continued the raven, a most dreadful year of drought in the elephants country, called the *Isles of Rad*, or of the *Wind*, insomuch that, pressed by extreme thirst, and not being able to come at any water, the whole body of the nation at length publicly addressed themselves to their king, beseeching him to apply some remedy to their misery, that they might not perish, or to destroy them all at once rather than let them endure a life of so much misery. The king, upon this passionate application, commanded diligent search to be made in all places in the neighbourhood, or at any reasonable distance: and at length there was discovered a spring of water; to which the ancients had given

the

the name of *Chafchmamah*, or the *Fountain of the Moon*. Immediately on this most happy difcovery, the king came and encamped with his whole army in the parts adjoining to this fountain: but, as misfortune would have it, the coming of the elephants ruined a great number of rabbits that had a warren in the same place, becaufe the elephants, every step they took, trod down their burroughs, and killed the poor creatures young ones.

The rabbits, on this public calamity, affembled together, went to their king, and befought him to deliver them from this terrible oppreffion. I know very well, anfwered the king, that I fit upon the throne only for the welfare and eafe of my fubjects; but, alas! you now ask me a thing that far furpaffeth my strength. Upon this one rabbit, more cunning than the reft, perceiving the king at a lofs, yet very much moved with the affliction of his people, ftept before his companions, and addreffing himfelf to the king; Sir, faid he, your majefty thinks like a juft and generous prince; while the care of our tranquillity difturbs your reft, and while you afford us the freedom to give our advice, it makes me bold to impart to your majefty an invention, lately come into my head, to drive thofe terrible deftroyers, the elephants, out of this country. Permit me only, continued the rabbit, that I may go with the character of your ambaffador to the king of the elephants, and doubt not but I will fend all thefe ftrangers away fafter than they came; neither need your majefty to fear that I shall make any improper fubmiffions to them; if any thought of that kind in the leaft difturbs your majefty's breaft, I am willing that your majesty should appoint me a companion, who may, at any time, return to you, and acquaint you with all that passes in my embassy.

No, replied the king, very obligingly, go alone and prosper; I will have no spies upon thy actions, for, I believe thee faithful; go, in the name of heaven, and do what thou shalt deem most convenient; only take care that you always remember that an ambassador is the king's tongue; his discourses therefore ought to be well weighed, and his words and his behaviour noble, and such as would suit the prince himself, whom he represents. The most learned in the kingdom ought always to be made choice of for ambassadors: nay, I have heard that one of the greatest monarchs in the world was wont frequently to disguise himself, and become his own ambassador. Indeed, for the honourable and proper discharge of that employment, the three necessary qualities are, resolution, eloquence, and a vast extent of natural parts. A violent spirit, let me tell you, is not fit for that employment. Several ambassadors, by a rash word, have created trouble in a peaceful kingdom: and others, with a mild and agreeable saying, have re-united irreconcileable enemies. Sir, said the rabbit, if I am not endowed with these good qualities your majesty has enumerated, I will endeavour, at least, to make the best of those I have; and shall ever remember this lesson which your majesty has honoured me with, and endeavour to act according to what your majesty has so justly declared to be the duty of one in so public and so honourable an employment.

Having

Having so said, he took his leave of the king, and went immediately forward on his journey to the elephants. Before he ventured himself among them, however, he bethought himself, that, if he went into the croud that usually attended on that king, he might very likely be trod to pieces: for which reason he got upon a high tree, whence he called to the king of the elephants, who was not far off, and addressed himself in the following words: I am, said he, the moon's ambassador; hear, therefore, with reverence and attention, what I have to say to you in her name: You, who in all ages have been famous for your adorations of your royal mistress, know full well, I doubt not, that the moon is a goddess whose power is unlimited, and, that above all things, she hates a lie.

The king of the elephants, who was a just and a most pious prince, trembled when he heard the rabbit talk of these things, and humbly desired to know the subject of his embassy. The moon, replied the rabbit, has sent me hither, to let you understand, that whoever is puffed up with his own grandeur, and despises her little ones, deserves death; and that she is grieved to see that you are not contented only to oppress the little ones, our peaceful and religious nation, but you have the insolence to trouble a fountain consecrated to her deity, where every thing is pure. Reform your manners, else you will be severely punished. And, if you will not give credit to my words, come and see the moon in her own fountain, and then, tremble and retire.

The king of the elephants was inwardly grieved and astonished at these words, and went to the fountain,

fountain, wherein he faw the moon indeed, becaufe the water was clear, and the moon then fhone very brightly. Then faid the rabbit to the elephant, you fee the facred deity; take of the water to wafh yourfelf, and pay your adorations. The elephant very obediently took fome of the water, but puddled the fountain with his trunk. At which the rabbit; Infidel, faid he, you have prophaned the fountain with your unhallowed touch; and, behold, the goddefs is gone away in a paffion! retire hence, therefore, I conjure you, with fpeed, with your whole army, left fome dreadful misfortune befal you. This threatening language put the king of the elephants into a trembling, and terrified him to that degree, that he prefently commanded his army to decamp, and away they all marched, never to return to the facred fountain of the moon again. And thus the rabbits were delivered from their enemies by the policy of one of their fociety.

I have only recited this example, continued the raven, to inftruct you, that you ought to make choice of a prudent and politic bird for your fovereign, fince by it you fee, that art and addrefs, even in the reprefentative of a king only, can do more than force in many cafes, though the king himfelf and his whole army engaged in the enterprife. Choofe, therefore, one for your king who may be able to affift you in your adverfities, and not an owl, who has neither courage nor wit. Thefe obfcene birds have nothing in them but malice, which will, one time or other, believe me, be no lefs fatal to you than the cat once was to the partridge, who defired him to decide a difference

ference which she had with another bird. The story is this.

## FABLE V.
### The CAT and the TWO BIRDS.

SOME years ago, continued the raven, I made my nest upon a tree, at the foot of which there frequently sat a partridge, a fair and comely bird, well-shaped and good-humoured. Our neighbouring situation soon brought us acquainted with one another; and, after a short knowledge of each other's talents and humour, we made a league of friendship together, and almost continually kept one another company. Some time after our first entering on this intimacy one with another, my friend, however, absented herself, for what reason I know not, and staid away so long, that I thought her dead; but my thoughts of this kind were erroneous; for, she at length returned, but had the misfortune to find her habitation in possession of another bird. The partridge pretended the house was hers, and would have made a forcible entry; but the bird refused to go out, alleging that possession was the strongest tenure of the law. I endeavoured soon after this to bring them to an accommodation; but all to no purpose; for, the partridge's attorney, finding she had money, urged her on, and tickled her ears with a lease of ejectment. However, at length, the partridge, finding the law to be very tedious and very expensive, said one day to herself, here lives hard by, I remember, a very devout

devout cat; she fasts every day, does nobody harm, and spends the nights in prayer; let us, in short, said she to her adversary, distract our brains and empty our purses no more about law, but refer our difference to her: I know not where we shall find a more equitable judge. The other bird having consented to this proposal, they went both to this religious cat, and I followed them out of curiosity. Entering, I saw the cat very attentive at a long prayer, without turning either to the right or left, which put me in mind of the old proverb, that, *long prayer before people is the key of hell.* I admired the sober hypocrisy, and had the patience to stay till the venerable personage had done. After which the partridge and his antagonist accosted him with great respect, and requested him to hear their difference, and give judgement according to the usual rules of justice. The cat, in his fur-gown, acting the part of a grave and formal judge, first heard what the stranger-bird had to plead for itself, and then addressing himself to the partridge, my pretty love, said he, come you now to me and let me hear your story; but, as I am old and thick of hearing, pray come near and lift up your voice, that I may not lose a word of what you say. The partridge and the other bird, on this, seeing him so devout and sanctified, both went boldly close up to him; but then the hypocrite discovered the bottom of his sanctity; for, he immediately fell upon them, and, in short, devoured them both.

You see by this example, continued he, that deceitful people are never to be trusted: and my inference from all this is, have you a care of the owl,

owl, who is in truth no better than the cat. The birds, convinced that the raven spoke nothing but what was reason, never minded the owl any more; and, upon this, the owl went home, meditating how to be revenged upon the raven, against whom he conceived such a mortal hatred, that time could never extinguish it.

This, sir, proceeded Carchenas, is the true reason of the perpetual enmity between us and the owls. I thank you, vizir, for this story, replied the monarch; and now let us consider what measures we must take to preserve the peace of my subjects, and revenge the affront I have received. To which Carchenas, making a low reverence, replied, Sir, permit me to speak my mind freely, and inform your majesty, that I am not of the same opinion with your other ministers, who advise either war, or flight, or an ignominious peace. I dissent from all, and would only recommend to your majesty to take at present no absolute resolution at all, but to follow cautiously this excellent maxim, That, when we want strength, we must have recourse to artifice and stratagem, and endeavour to deceive the enemy, by feigning one thing and doing another. The advantage of this way of proceeding, in things of this kind, we may see by the following example.

FABLE

## FABLE VI.

### The DERVISE *and the* FOUR ROBBERS.

A Dervise had once made a purchase of a fine fat sheep, with intent to offer it up in sacrifice; and, having tied a chord about the neck of it, was leading it to his habitation; but, as he led it along, four thieves perceived him, and had a great mind to steal his sacrifice for less holy uses. They dared not, however, take it away from the dervise by force, because they were too near the city, therefore they made use of this stratagem; they first parted company, and then accosted the dervise, whom they knew to be an honest and inoffensive man, and one who thought of no more harm in others than he had in himself, as if they had come from several distinct parts. Said the first of them, who had contrived to meet him full-face, Father, whither are you leading this dog? At this instant the second coming from another quarter, cried to him, Venerable old gentleman, I hope you have not so far forgot yourself as to have stolen this dog. And immediately after him the third coming up and asking him, Whither he would go coursing with that handsome grey-hound? the poor dervise began to doubt whether the sheep, which he had, was a sheep or not. But the fourth robber put him quite beside himself, coming up at that instant, and saying to him, Pray, reverend father, what did this dog cost you? The dervise, on this, absolutely persuaded that four men, coming from four several places, could not all be deceived,

verily

verily believed that the grasier who had sold him the sheep was a conjurer, and had bewitched his sight; insomuch that, no longer giving credit to his own eyes, he began to be firmly convinced that the sheep he was leading was a dog; and, immediately, in full persuasion of it, went back to the market to demand his money of the grasier, leaving the wether with the felons, who carried it away.

Sir, said Carchenas, your majesty sees, by this example, that what cannot be done by force must be atchieved by policy. You advise me well, said the king; but now tell me by what invention shall we revenge ourselves on the owls? Rely upon me, replied Carchenas, to take care of your majesty's revenge, and suffer me to sacrifice my own private ease to the public good. Only order my feathers to be pulled off, and leave me all over bloody under this tree, and doubt not but I will do you an acceptable service. It was no small grief to Birouz to give out such a cruel order in regard to this excellent minister, however, at his own inceffant entreaties, the thing at length was done, and the king marched away with his army to wait for Carchenas in a place where that vizir had appointed him.

In the mean time night came, and the owls, puffed up with the success of their insolence the night before, returned, intending now, by a bloody battle, at once to complete the destruction of the ravens. But they were amazed when they missed the enemy, whom they intended to have surprised. They sought for the raven's army diligently from every corner, and in their

searches

searches they heard a voice of grevous lamentation, which was the voice of Carchenas who was lamenting at the foot of a tree. The king of the owls on this immediately approached him, and examined him concerning his birth, and the employment he had in Birouz's court? Alas! replied Carchenas, the condition in which you see me sufficiently shews you my inability to give you the account which you demand. I have not strength, alas! to repeat it. What crime did you commit then, replied Chabahang, to deserve this hard usage? No crime, O mighty monarch! replied Carchenas; but the wicked ravens, upon a slight suspicion only, have used me thus. After our army, continued he, was thrown into terror and affright last night by your bold defiance, king Birouz called a council, to seek out ways to be revenged of so heinous an affront: and, after he had heard the various opinions of some of his ministers, he commanded me to speak mine: at which time I laid before him, that you were not only superior in number, but better disciplined, and more valiant than we were; and by consequence that it was necessary for us to desire peace, and to accept of whatever conditions you would be pleased to grant us. This so incensed the king against me, that, in a violent passion, Traitor, cried he, this is the way to infuse into my army a fear of the enemy, by exalting their strength and lessening mine; and with that, suspecting that I was meditating to seek my peace with your majesty, he commanded that I should be used as you see.

After Carchenas had done speaking, the king of the owls asked his chief minister what was to be
done

done with him? The only way, sir, answered the minister is to put him out of his pain, and knock him on the head; never trust his fair speeches, for I do not believe a word he says. Remember the old proverb, sir, *the more dead, the fewer enemies.* Carchenas, on this, in a lamentable tone, cried out, I beseech you, sir, add not to my affliction by your threatening language.

The king of the owls, who could not choose but compassionate Carchenas, now bid the second minister speak; who was not of the first vizir's opinion. Sir, said he, I would not advise your majesty to put this person to death. Kings ought to assist the weak, and succour those that throw themselves into their protection. Besides, continued he, sometimes there may be great advantage made of an enemy's service, according to the story of a certain merchant, which, with permission, I will relate to your majesty.

## FABLE VII.

### The MERCHANT, his WIFE, and the ROBBER.

THERE was once, continued the minister, a certain merchant, very rich, but homely, and very deformed in his person, who had married a very fair and virtuous wife. He loved her passionately; but, on the other hand, she hated him; insomuch that, not being able to endure

dure him, she lay by herself in a separate bed in the same chamber.

It happened, soon after they were married, that a thief one night broke into the house, and came into the chamber. The husband was at this time asleep; but the wife, being awake, and perceiving the thief, was in such a terrible fright, that she ran to her husband, and caught him fast in her arms. The husband, waking, was transported with joy to see the delight of his life clasping him in her embraces. Bless me! cried he, to what am I obliged for this extraordinary happiness? I wish I knew the person to whom I owe it, that I might return him thanks. Hardly had he uttered the words, when the thief appeared, and he soon guessed the whole occasion. Oh! cried the merchant, the most welcome person in the world; take whatever thou thinkest fitting, I cannot reward thee sufficiently for the good service thou hast done me.

By this example we may see that our enemies may sometimes be serviceable to us, in obtaining those things which we have sought in vain to enjoy by the help of our friends. So that, since this raven may prove beneficial to us, we ought, I am of opinion, to preserve his life.

The king, on this minister's ending his speech, asked a third what he thought; who delivered his opinion in these words. Sir, said he, so far from putting this raven to death, you ought to caress him, and engage him by your favours to do you some important service. The wise always endeavour to oblige some of their enemies, in order to set up a faction against the rest, and then

then make advantage of their divisions. The quarrel, which the devil once had with the thief, was the reason that neither the one nor the other could hurt a very virtuous dervise, according to the ensuing fable.

## FABLE VIII.

*The* DERVISE, *the* THIEF, *and the* DEVIL.

IN the parts adjoining to Babylon, continued the third minister, there was once a certain dervise, who lived like a true servant of heaven: he subsisted only upon such alms as he received; and, as for other things, gave himself up wholly to providence, without troubling his mind with the intrigues of this world.

One of the friends of this dervise, one day, sent him a fat ox; which a thief seeing as it was led to his lodging, resolved to have it whatever it cost him. With this intent he set forward for the dervise's habitation; but, as he went on, he met the devil in the shape of a plain-dressed man, and, suspecting by his countenance that he was one of his own stamp, he immediately asked him who he was and whither he was going? The stranger, on this, made a short answer to his demand, saying, I am the devil, who have taken human shape upon me, and I am going to this cave, with intent to kill the dervise that lives there; because his example does me a world of mischief, by making several wicked people turn honest and good men: I intend, therefore, to put him out of the way, and then hope to succeed

better

better in my business than I have done of late; else I assure you we shall soon want people in my dominions. Mr. Satan, answered the thief, I am your most obedient humble servant; I assure you I am one you have no reason to complain about, for I am a notorious robber, and am going to the same place whither you are bent, to steal a fat ox, that was, a few hours ago, given to the dervise that you design to kill. My good friend, quoth the devil, I am heartily glad I have met you, and rejoice that we are both of the same humour, and that both of us design to do this abominable dervise a mischief. Go on and prosper, continued the devil, and know, when you rob such people as these, you do me a doubly-acceptable service.

In the midst of this discourse they came both to the dervise's habitation; night was already well advanced; and the good man had said his usual prayers, and was gone to bed. And now the thief and the devil were both preparing to put their designs in execution; when the thief said to himself, the devil in going to kill this man will certainly make him cry out, and raise the neighbourhood, which will hinder me from stealing the ox. The devil, on the other hand, reasoned with himself after this manner: If the thief goes to steal the ox before I have executed my design, the noise he will make in breaking open the door will awaken the dervise, and set him on his guard. Therefore said the devil to the thief, let me first kill the dervise, and then thou mayest steal the ox at thy own leisure; no, said the thief, the better way will be for you to stay till I have stolen the ox, and

then

then do you murder the man. But, both refusing to give way the one to the other, they quarrelled first, and from words they fell to downright fisty-cuffs. At which sport the devil proving the stronger of the two, the thief called out to the dervise, Awake, man, arise, here is the devil come to murder you. And, on this, the devil, perceiving himself discovered, cried out, Thieves, thieves, look to your ox, dervise. The good man, quickly waking at the noise, called in the neighbours, whose presence constrained the thief and the devil to betake themselves to their heels: and the poor dervise saved both his life and his ox.

The chief minister, having heard this fable, falling into a very great passion, said to the king, Listen not, O sacred sir, I beseech you, to these idle stories: if you give way to what they would insinuate, believe me, you will suffer yourself to be deceived by this raven, not less than the joiner was deceived by his wife. What is that story? replied Chabahang, go on and relate it to me.

## FABLE IX.

### The JOINER and his WIFE.

IN the city of Guaschalla, sir, continued the minister then, there once lived a joiner, who was very skilful in his art, and the husband of a wife so beautiful, that the sun seemed to borrow his brightness from her eyes; and she was so passionately

sionately beloved by her husband, that he was almost out of his wits when he was constrained to be absent but for a moment from her. This fine lady, on her part, was so crafty, that she had found the way to make her husband believe she loved him as dearly as he did her, and had no pleasure but in his company, though at the same time she had several gallants that were not unacceptable to her. Among the rest there was a neighbour of hers, a young man, well shaped, and with a good face, who had won her affection to that degree that she began to care for none of the rest. Upon which they became so jealous of him, that, despairing of any good luck for themselves, in revenge, they gave the joiner notice of his familiarity with his wife. The honest husband, however, was unwilling to believe any thing, unless he were well assured; and, therefore, that he might be certain of a truth which he was yet afraid to know, he pretended one day that he was to go a small journey; and, taking some provisions with him, told his wife that it was true he should not go very far, but his business he was afraid would keep him out two or three days; and, that it would be a great trouble to him to want her company so long; but that he must endeavour to support himself under it with the thoughts of her goodness. His wife paid him in the same coin, bemoaning the tediousness of his absence, and shedding an April shower of tears rather for joy than grief. The lady soon got every thing ready for her husband's departure; and he, the better to dissemble the matter, bid her be sure to keep the doors fast for fear of thieves. She, on the other side, promised to be

very

very careful of every thing, and still put on a show of the deepest melancholy, for grief that he was to leave her. Her husband's back was no sooner turned, however, but she gave notice to her gallant to come to her, who kept his time to a minute: in short, he was there before the joiner was well gone, and a world of happiness they were fondly promising themselves. But, while they were dallying together, the joiner returned home, entered without being seen, and clapt himself into a corner to see how things went.

The gallant now, every moment, most eagerly caressed his mistress, who admitted his fondnesses with delight. In fine, they supped together, and then made themselves ready to go to bed.

The joiner, who, till then, had seen nothing that could perfectly convince him of his shame, stole softly toward the bed, intending to take them in the act; but his wife, having now luckily observed him, whispered her lover in the ear that he should ask her which she loved best, him or her husband. Presently her gallant, with a loud voice, Do not you love me, my dear, cried he, much better than your husband? Why do you ask me so foolish a question? answered the wife: know you not that women, when they seem to shew any friendship to any other man but their husbands, only do it to satisfy their pleasure; and, when they are satisfied, never think of their pretended lover more? for my part, I assure you I idolize my husband, I wear him always in my heart; and, in my opinion, indeed, that woman is unworthy to live, that loves not her husband better than herself.

These

These words were some kind of cordial to the joiner's spirits, who began now to blame himself for the bad opinion he had just before entertained of his wife; saying to himself, the fault which she now commits must be imputed to my absence and the frailty of her sex: the chastest person in the world sins either in deed or intention; and therefore, since she loves me so well, I cannot but pardon her offence, nor will I be so cruel to deprive her of a moment of her pleasure. After he had made these reflections, the courteous spouse retired to his corner, and let the two lovers wanton together all the rest of the night, which they did not without some fear on the lady's side, who, when she saw no more of her husband, thought her eyes had deceived her, and ventured to bed, but was not, however, without some panics.

After a night thus spent, the lover, early in the morning, arose and departed, and the wife lay in bed counterfeiting herself asleep. When the husband, going to bed in his turn, fell to kissing and caressing her; and the wife, opening her eyes and dissembling astonishment, Laud! my dear heart, said she to her husband, how long have you been returned? Why, I have been returned ever since last night, replied the joiner, but I was unwilling to disturb the young man that lay with you, because I perceived that you had me in your mind all the while you received his caresses, which you would never have admitted but that you thought me absent. Upon these kind words, the wife, frankly and with a seeming openness of heart, confessed her fault, and begged him never to be absent again.

This

This example inſtructs us, ſir, that we are not to be lulled aſleep with fair words. Enemies, when they cannot attain their ends by force, commonly have recourſe to artifices, and humble themſelves to deceive us. Here Carchenas cried out, Oh! you that are ſo zealous for my death, why do you not put an end at once to my days, but talk ſo many things to no purpoſe to increaſe my miſery? what probability is there of perfidiouſneſs in a perſon ſo wounded as I am? what madman would ſuffer ſo much torment to do good to another? It is in that very thing, replied the vizir, that thy ſubtilty conſiſts. The ſweetneſs of revenge, which thou art meditating, makes thee patiently ſwallow the bitterneſs of thy pains. Thou wouldſt fain make thyſelf as famous as the monkey that ſacrificed his life to the ſafety of his country. I moſt humbly entreat the king to to hear the ſtory.

## FABLE X.

### *The* MONKEYS *and the* BEARS.

A Great number of monkeys once, continued he, lived in a country well ſtored with all manner of fruit, and very delightful. It happened one day a bear travelling that way by accident, and conſidering the beauty of the reſidence, and the ſweet lives the monkeys led, ſaid to himſelf, it is not juſt or reaſonable that theſe little animals ſhould live ſo happy, while I am forced to run through foreſts and mountains in ſearch

search of food. Full of indignation at this difference of fortune, he ran immediately among the apes, and killed some of them for very madness: but they all fell upon him; and, in regard they were very numerous, they soon made him all over wounds, so that he had much ado to make his escape.

Thus punished for his rashness, he made what haste he could to escape, and at length recovered a mountain within hearing of some of his comrades; and no sooner saw himself there, but he set up a loud roaring, that a great number of bears immediately came about him, to whom he recounted what had befallen him. When they had heard the story out, instead of the emotions he expected to have found in them, they all laughed at him: Thou art a most wretched coward, cried they, to suffer thyself to be beaten by those little animals. This is true, indeed, replied a leading bear, but, however, this affront is not to be endured; it must be revenged for the honour of our nation. On this they soon concerted proper measures to annoy the enemy; and, towards the beginning of the night, descended all from the mountain, and fell pell-mell upon the monkeys, who were dreaming of nothing less than of such an invasion; in short, they were all retired to their rest, when they were surrounded by the bears, who killed a great number, the rest escaping in disorder. After this exploit, the bears were so taken with this habitation, that they made choice of it for the place of their own settled abode. They set up, for their king, the bear that had been so ill handled by the monkeys; and, after that, fell to banquet upon the

provisions

provisions which the monkeys had heaped together in their magazines.

The next morning, by break of the day, the king of the monkeys (who knew nothing of this fatal calamity, for he had been hunting for two days together) met several monkeys maimed, who gave him an account of what had passed the day before. The king, when he heard the doleful news, immediately began to weep and lament the vast treasure he had lost, accusing heaven of injustice, and fortune of inconstancy. In the midst of all his indignation and sorrow, his subjects also pressed him to take his revenge; so that the poor king knew not which way to turn himself. Now, among the monkeys, that at that time attended on this monarch, there was one called Maimon, who was one of the most crafty and most learned in the court, and was the king's chief favourite. This poor creature, seeing his master sad, and his companions in consternation, stood up, and addressing himself to the king: Persons of wit and discretion, said he, never abandon themselves to despair, which is a tree that bears very bad fruit; but patience, on the contrary, supplies us with a thousand inventions to rid ourselves from the intanglements of trouble and adversity.

The king, whom this discourse had rendered much more easy in his mind, turning to Maimon, on this, said, But how shall we do, vizir, to bring ourselves off with honour from this ignominious misfortune? Maimon besought his majesty, on this, to allow him private audience; and, after he had obtained it, he spoke to this effect.

Sir, said he, I conjure you, by the dear hopes of a great revenge, to hear me out with patience. My heart is as much distracted, O my sacred master, for my private, if it be possible, as for the public, misfortune: my wife and children have been massacred by these tyrants. Imagine, then, my grief to see myself deprived for ever of those sweets, which I enjoyed in the society of my family: and hear me with patience, and full belief, when I assure you I have resolved to die, that I may put an end to my sorrows: but my death shall not be idle; no, I will find means to make it prove fatal to my royal master's enemies. O Maimon, said the king, consider, we never desire to be revenged of our enemies but with intent to procure to ourselves repose or satisfaction of mind; but, when you are dead, what signifies it to you whether the world be at war or in peace? Sir, replied Maimon, in the condition I am in, life being insupportable to me, I sacrifice it with delight to the happiness of my companions. All the favour I beg of your majesty is, only with gratitude and compassion to remember my generosity when you shall be re-established in your dominions. What I have farther to ask of you is this, that you will immediately command my ears to be torn from my head, my teeth to be pulled out, and my feet to be cut off; and then let me be left for the night in a corner of the forest where we were lodged; then retire yo*, sir, with the remainder of your subjects, and remove two days journey hence, and, on the third, you may return to your palace; for, you shall hear no more of your enemies; and may you for

ever

ever reap the bleſſings my death intends you. The king, though with great grief, cauſed Maimon's deſires to be executed, and left him in the wood, where all night be made the moſt doleful lamentations that ever miſery uttered.

When day ſhone out, the king of the bears, who had all night long heard Maimon's outcries, advanced to ſee what miſerable creature had made the noiſe; and, beholding the poor monkey in that condition, he was moved with compaſſion, notwithſtanding his merciless humour, and aſked him who he was, and who had uſed him after that barbarous manner? Maimon, judging by all appearances that he was the king of the bears that ſpoke to him, after he had reſpectfully ſaluted him, expreſſed himſelf in the following words: Sir, ſaid he, I am the king of the monkeys' chief miniſter; I went, ſome days ago, hunting with him, and at our return, underſtanding the ravages which your majeſty's ſoldiers had committed in our houſes, he took me aſide, and aſked me what was his beſt courſe to take at ſuch a juncture? I anſwered him, without any heſitation, that we ought to put ourſelves under your protection, that we might live at eaſe, and unmoleſted. The king, my maſter, then talked many ridiculous things of your majeſty, which was the reaſon that I took the boldneſs to tell him, that you were a moſt renowned prince, and, beyond all compariſon, more potent than he; which audaciouſneſs of mine incenſed him to that degree, that immediately he commanded me to be thus mangled, as you ſee me.

Maimon had no ſooner concluded his relation, but he let fall ſuch a ſhower of tears, that the king

king of the bears was mollified also, and could not forbear weaping himself. When this was a little over, he asked Maimon, where the monkeys were. In a desart called Mardazmay, answered he, where they are raising a prodigious army, the whole place, for a thousand leagues extent, being inhabited by no other creatures but monkeys; and there is no question to me made but they will be with you in a very short time. The king of the bears, not a little terrified at the news, asked Maimon, whom he thought sufficiently exasperated against the monkey-government to make him his assured friend, what course he should take to secure himself from the enterprises of the monkeys. Face them boldly, replied Maimon, your majesty need not fear them; were not my legs broke, I would undertake with one single troop of your forces to destroy forty thousand of them. You advise me well, said the king, and, with your help, I doubt not but I shall destroy them. There is no question but you know all the avenues to their camp. You will oblige us for ever, would you but conduct us thither; and be assured we will revenge the barbarity committed upon your person. That, alas! is impossible, replied Maimon, because I can neither go nor stand. There is a remedy for every thing, answered the king, and I will find an invention to carry you; and, at the same time, he gave orders to his army to be in readiness to march, and to put themselves into a condition to fight. They all readily obeyed the orders, and tied Maimon, who was to be their guide, upon the head of one of the biggest bears.

Maimon

Maimon now gloried in his mind that he had it in his power to revenge all that himself and his country had suffered. And, in order to it, conducted them into the defart of Mardazmay, where there blew a poifonous wind, and where the heat was fo vehement, that no creature could live an hour in it. Now, when the bears were entered into the borders of this dangerous defart, Maimon, to engage them farther into it, Come, faid he, let us make hafte and furprife thefe accurfed wretches before day. With fuch exhortations he kept them on the march all night; but, the next day, they were aftonifhed to find themfelves in fo difmal a place. They not only did not fee, fo much as the likenefs of a monkey, but they perceived that the fun had fo heated the air, that the very birds that flew over the defart fell down, as it were, roafted to death; and the fand was fo burning hot, that the bears feet were all burned to the bones. The king, on this, cried out to Maimon, into what a defart haft thou brought us? and what fierce whirlwinds are thefe which I fee coming towards us? On this the monkey, finding they were all too far advanced for the leaft poffibility of getting back, and therefore fure to perifh, fpoke boldly; and, in anfwer to the king of the bears, Tyrant, faid he, know that we are in the defart of death; the whirlwind that approaches us is death itfelf, which comes in a moment to punifh thee for all thy cruelties. And, while he was thus fpeaking, the fiery whirlwind came and fwept them all away.

Two days after this, the king of the monkeys returned to his palace, as Maimon foretold him; and,

and, finding all his enemies gone, continued a long reign in peace over his subjects.

Your majesty, pursued the vizir, sees, by this example, that there is no trusting to the alluring words of an enemy. And, permit me to add, that he ought to perish that seeks the destruction of others. This discourse, continued so positively, put the king of the owls in a passion; insomuch, that he cried to the chief minister, Why all this stir to hinder this poor miserable creature from the proof of my clemency? and, at the same time, commanded his surgeons to dress Carchenas, and to take particular care of him. You do not consider, added the king, that yourself may one time fall into as great afflictions as have now befallen him.

Carchenas was now dressed, and taken care of, by the king's own surgeon, who soon recovered him from his wounds. And, when he was able to stir about, he behaved himself so well, that, in a little time, he won the love of all the court. The king of the owls confided absolutely in him, and began to do nothing without first consulting him. One day, Carchenas, addressing himself to the king; Sir, said he, the king of the ravens has abused me so unjustly, that I shall never die satisfied unless I have first gratified my revenge. I have been a long time endeavouring to contrive the means, but find, as the result of all my studies about it, that I never can compass it safely nor absolutely, so long as I wear the shape of a raven. I have heard, I remember, persons of learning and experience say, that he who has been ill
used

used by a tyrant, if he make any wish by way of revenge, must, if he would have it succeed, throw himself into the fire; for that, while he continues there, all his wishes will be heard. For this reason I beseech your majesty that I may be thrown into the fire, to the end that, in the middle of the flames, I may beg of heaven to change me into an owl: perhaps heaven will hear my prayer, and then, I doubt not, but I shall be able to revenge myself upon the enemy.

The chief minister, that had always spoken against Carchenas, was then in the assembly, and, hearing this insinuating speech, O traitor, cried he, whither tends all this superfluous language? Now, do I full well know that thou art weaving mischief, though I cannot divine of what kind it will be; but the event, I know, will shew it. Sir, added he, turning to the king, caress this wicked fellow as long as you please, he will never change his nature. Does not your majesty remember that the mouse was once metamorphosed into a maid; and yet she could not forbear wishing to have a rat for her husband. You love fables dearly, vizir, said the king to him, and I will indulge you in your pleasure. and hear this willingly; but I will not promise you to be a pin. the better for it.

FABLE

## FABLE XI.

### The MOUSE *that was changed into a* LITTLE GIRL.

A Person of quality, continued the vizir, once, walking by the side of a fountain, saw a very beautiful little mouse fall at his feet from the bill of a raven, who held it a little too carelessly. The gentleman, out of pity, and pleased with its beauty, took it up, and carried it home; but, fearing it should cause disorder in the family, as the women are generally not very fond of these animals, he prayed to heaven to change it into a maid. The prayer came from the mouth of a person of so much piety and goodness, that it was heard; and what he requested was presently done; so that, instead of a mouse, on a sudden he saw before him a very pretty little girl, whom he afterwards bred up. Some years after, the good man seeing his foster-child big enough to be married, Choose out, said he to her, in the whole extent of this country, the creature that pleases thee best, and I will make him thy husband; for I can give thee a fortune which will make any body glad to offer his service to thee. If I may choose, sir, for myself, in so important an affair, replied the maid, let me acknowledge to you that I am very ambitious. I would, continued she, have a husband so strong, that he should never be vanquished. That must needs be the sun, replied the old gentleman; it is a strange desire,

desire, child; but, however, thou shalt not want my best offices in it: and, therefore, the next morning, said he to the sun, my daughter desires an invincible husband, will you marry her? Alas! answered the sun, call not me invincible, yonder cloud enfeebles my beams; address yourself to that. The good man, on this, turned and made his compliment to the cloud. Alas! said the cloud, the wind drives me as it pleases. The old gentleman, nothing discouraged, desired the wind to marry his daughter. But the wind, laying before him that his strength was stopped by such a mountain, he addressed himself to the mountain. O sir, said the mountain, the rat is stronger than I, for he pierces me in every side, and eats into my very bowels; whereupon the old gentleman, in great sorrow of heart, went at length to the rat, who liked very well the proposal, and immediately consented to marry his daughter, saying, withal, that he had been a long time seeking out for a wife. The old gentleman, on this, returning home, asked his daughter whether she would be contented to marry a rat? Now he expected that she would have abhorred the thoughts of such a marriage; but was amazed to see her out of patience to be united to this precious husband. Thereupon, the old man, with great sorrow, cried out, Nothing, I find, can alter nature. In fine he went to his prayers again, and desired of heaven, that it would again turn his daughter into a mouse, as she was before; which it accordingly did, and put an end to his care.

The king of the owls heard this, and whatever else the vizir had to say, with great patience; but, attributing all the remonstrances to his jealousy of the raven, took little notice of them. In the mean time, Carchenas, who was all this time a courtier, and the principal favourite of the king, had an opportunity to observe all the comings and goings-out of the owls, and whatever else it might be of service to his country to know: and, when he had perfectly informed himself of every thing, he fairly left them, and returned to the ravens. On his arrival in the raven camp, he gave the king, his master, an account of every thing that had passed, and said, Now, sir, is the time for us to be revenged of our enemies; and what I have seen among them teaches me how it may be effected. In a certain mountain, that I know of, and can in a day's march lead you to, there is a cave where all the nation of the owls meet every day. Now, as this mountain is environed with wood, your majesty needs no more but to command your army to carry a great quantity of that wood to the mouth of the cave. I will be ready at hand to kindle the wood, and then let all the ravens flutter round about to blow the fire into a flame: by this means such owls as shall adventure out will be burned in the flames, and such as stay within shall be smothered; and so shall your majesty be delivered at once from all your enemies.

The king highly approved the raven's counsel, adored his courage and address in his adventurous enterprize, by which he had learned this; and, ordering his whole army to set forward

ward, they did as Carchenas had contrived, and, by that means, deftroyed at one inftant all the owls of the neighbouring nation.

By this example we may fee, that fometimes fubmiffion to an enemy is requifite for the eluding of their wicked defigns: of which the fable that follows is yet a farther proof.

---

## FABLE XII.

### *The* SERPENT *and the* FROGS.

A Certain ferpent once became old and feeble and no longer able to hunt abroad for his food. In this unfortunate condition, long he bewailed in folitude the infirmities of age, and wifhed in vain for the ftrength of his youthful years. Hunger, at length, however, taught him, inftead of his lamentations, a ftratagem to get his livelihood. He went flowly on to the brink of a ditch, in which there lived an infinite number of frogs, that had juft then elected a king to rule over them. Arrived at this fcene of delight, the wily ferpent feemed to be very fad, and extremely fick; upon which a frog popped up his head, and afked him what he ailed? I am ready to ftarve, anfwered the ferpent; formerly I lived upon the creatures of your fpecies which I was able to take, but now I am fo unfortunate, that I cannot catch any thing to fubfift on. The frogs,

on

on this account, went and informed the king of the serpent's condition, and his answer to the question he asked him. Upon which report, the king went himself to the place to look upon the serpent; who seeing him, Sir, said he, one day, as I was going to snap a frog by the foot, he got from me, and fled before me to a certain dervise's apartment, and there entered into a dark chamber, in which there lay a little infant asleep. At the same time I also entered, in pursuit of my game, and, feeling the child's foot, which I took for the frog, I bit it in such a venomous manner, that the infant immediately died. The dervise, on this, provoked by my boldness, pursued me with all his might; but, not being able to overtake me, he fell upon his knees, and begged of heaven, for the punishment of my crime, that I might never be able to catch frogs more, that I might perish with hunger, unless their king gave me one or two in charity; and, lastly, he added to his wishes, that I might be their slave and obey them. These prayers of the dervise, continued the serpent, were heard, and I am now come, since it is the will of heaven, to submit myself to your laws, and obey your orders as long as I live.

The king of the frogs received his submissive enemy, with an acceptance of his services; but, at the same time, it was with great disdain and swelling pride, that he told him, with a haughty taunt, that he would not disobey the heavens, but would make use of his service: and, accordingly, the serpent got into employment, and, for some days, carried the king upon his back; but, at length,

Most

Most potent monarch, said he, if you intend that I should serve you long, you must feed me, else I shall starve to death. Thou sayest very true, honest serpent, replied the king of the frogs, henceforward I allow thee to swallow two of my subjects a day for thy subsistence. And this was all he had to wish for. Thus the serpent, by submitting to his enemy, secured to himself, at his cost, a comfortable subsistence during the remainder of his life.

To conclude, most sacred sir, said Pilpay, your majesty sees, by these examples, that patience is a noble virtue, and that it greatly conduces to bring about vast designs. The wise men of old, sir, had sufficient reason to say, that prudence goes beyond strength: and your majesty may see, by what I have related, that a man, by his wit, may often redeem himself out of danger. But your majesty is also to remember, that these examples often inform us, that we are never to trust an enemy, whatever protestations of friendship he makes; for, in spite of all the fair speeches in the world, we ought to know that a raven will be a raven still. *True friends* only are, therefore, to be relied upon; and the conversation and familiarity of such alone can be truly beneficial to us.

## THE END.

www.ingramcontent.com/pod-product-compliance
Lightning Source LLC
Chambersburg PA
CBHW032100220426
43664CB00008B/1072